M0762

ICE BREAKERS 2
64 MORE
GAMES AND FUN ACTIVITIES

by
Valerie Lippoldt Mack

To Greg Gilpin, thanks for believing I had more games in me.
To Stevie and Zane, thanks for thinking mom's games are still cool.
To Anissa Sanborn and Nancy Wesche, thanks for proofing and trying all the games.
And to my incredible husband, Tom, thanks for having faith in me and my games.

Lastly, thank you to all my students and friends
who have allowed me my games.

and the silver box blessings!

Shawnee Press

EXCLUSIVELY DISTRIBUTED BY

HAL•LEONARD®
CORPORATION
7777 W. BLUEMOUND RD. P.O. BOX 13819 MILWAUKEE, WI 53213

Visit Shawnee Press Online at www.shawneepress.com

foreword...4

icebreakers - remixed!
Says Simon...5
Move It Out!...6
Folder Scramble...7
Ba-da Bingo...8
Flying Fish...9
On Your Mark...10
Leader of the Pack.......................................11
Kiki's Whoppit Game......................................12
ABC Art (Already Been Chewed!)...........................13
Standing O...14

stress busters - solving problems as a team
Power Extension..15
Top Hat and Cane...16
Patterns...17
Musical Digits...18
Score or No Score..19
"Is a Puzzlement".......................................20
Top Ten Arguments..21
Smash Mouth..22
Marsh-Ball...23
Ping-Pong Pitch..24
Balloon Busters..25

creative activities - thinking outside the box
Ice Cubes and Chopsticks.................................26
Topsy Turvy..27
Human Machines...28
What Comes After Ti?.....................................29
Same Name Fame Game......................................30
Initial That...31
Suo I Codilai Pxecit.....................................32
Crayon Box...33
Musical Trip...34
House of Cards...35
Cent-sational Listening..................................36

table of contents

IceBreakers 2: 64 MORE Games and Fun Activities

retreat makers - building relationships

Can You Hear Me Now? 37
Label Fable 38
"To Be or Not To Be?" 39
Tapestry 40
Simu-relations 41
Warm Fuzzies 42
Venn Connections 43
Nature Calls 44
Heads Up! Singer's Up! 45
Bravissimo! 46
Break-a-leg Ideas 47

life lessons - establishing respect

What's Your Ring Tone? 48
Meaningful Initials 49
Don't Squash My Butterfly! 50
Energizing Envelopes 51
Talent Chain 52
Nicknames 53
Iceland or Bust 54
More Headliner Questions 55
Silver Trophies 56

holiday games - celebrating special occasions

New Year's "Party Time" (January) 57
Valentine Cut-outs (February) 58
Land O' Green (March) 59
Egg-citing Egg Hunt (March or April) 60
April Falling Fools (April) 61
Birthday Bash (Any month) 62
Firecracker Dance (July) 63
Ghoulish Game (October) 64
Thankful Turkey Trot (November) 65
The Gift Goes On (December) 66
Holiday Parade (Any month) 67
Wrap It Up! (Any month) 68

50 Suggested Song and Dance Titles for "Move It Out" 69
Author's Bio 71

To indicate that this book is intended for all people, the publisher alternates between masculine and feminine pronouns throughout the book.

I C E B R E A K E R S

foreword

IceBreakers: 60 Fun Activities That Will Build a Better Choir! was my first resource book based on games and activities for music educators. I successfully used these ideas in my own musicclassroom and they were received with such great enthusiasm that my next book, ***IceBreakers 2: 64 MORE Games and Fun Activities*** was born. My students, teacher-friends, and my children, Stevie and Zane, were the inspiration for many of these games. There are new categories in ***IceBreakers 2*** including a holiday section with icebreaker games for special celebrations or retreats.

This year, I presented many ***Icebreaker*** workshops and each time the same remarkable phenomenon occurred – participants were always rejuvenated and energized. Teachers were not only enjoying in-services, but were jumping out of their seats to participate! Suddenly students were focused throughout entire rehearsals! From the responses I have received, the games are working for students, educators, and musicians around the world.

Shortly after the first ***Icebreaker*** book was published, I had the privilege of being interviewed by Aled Jones of the British Broadcast Corporation. Aled, with his charming British accent, asked how American teachers find time to play games during music rehearsals. I responded, "How can you not take the time? In each game you play and each song you sing, you are teaching a lesson! Icebreaker activities generate focus, create energy, and build teamwork. You had better believe I have my ***Icebreakers*** book ready EVERY TIME I walk into a rehearsal! I have to have a few tricks up my sleeve to maintain that 'rehearsal magic.' Some days, it is imperative to change the direction of the rehearsal as soon as students walk into the classroom." Aled was so enthralled with this notion that by the end of the interview, he asked me where he could get a copy of ***Icebreakers*** for his own library.

Educators and administrators need to appreciate and celebrate each and every member of the team. Students need a place to belong – a family away from home. The more you demonstrate to your students that you care and respect them as individuals, the more they will care and respect you and your music program in return. Let's face it, your classroom just might be the only "home" some of your students know.

And now, let the games begin…
~ *Valerie Lippoldt Mack (2009)*

"You can discover more about a person in an hour of play than in a year of conversation."
~ *Plato* (400 B.C.)

says simon

PURPOSE:
One of the most important skills students must learn is to pay attention to directions. Even when students think they "know the ropes," they still need to focus and listen carefully without automatically going into autopilot mode. **Says Simon** is a silly activity that will convince students to pay attention by thinking in opposites!

REQUIREMENTS:
Room to move • Masking tape (for variations of the game)

PREPARATION:
Brush up on the rules for the childhood game, "Simon Says," and write each directive down...only preparing it backwards so you don't forget the word order in the heat of battle.

DIRECTIONS:
1. Explain to the class that the "Simon" will call out simple commands. The twist of this icebreaker is that the playing students must interpret the directions backwards! For example, if the leader says, "Says Simon, touch your toes," the players SHOULD NOT touch his toes. But, if the leader says simply, "Touch your toes," (without the "Simon"), the players SHOULD touch his toes. This sounds simple enough, but if the leader exclaims, "Says Simon...," the players do not follow instructions in order to stay in the game and avoid elimination.
2. Ask for a volunteer "Simon" to call out directives...who will start with simple commands.
3. Tell the students to spread out to use all available space to move around.
4. The goal is to remain in the game while retraining your students' brains from automatically following the childhood game rules of "Simon Says."
5. The students will have to make every effort to "be present" and listen carefully to avoid elimination.
6. Designate a winner who successfully played backwards as the new "Simon" to call out backwards directions for the next round of the game.

VARIATIONS:
- **Rover Red** Similar to the **Says Simon** activity above, **Rover Red** is also played in a backwards manner. If the first team says, "Rover Red, Rover Red, send all the guys over instead," the entire class of girls would run over the other side (not the guys). If the leader calls for anyone wearing red to go to the other side, those wearing red should remain in their places. Students who are not wearing red clothing or shoes will run to the other side.
- **Pink Light**, **Purple Light** Students run when the leader says "pink light" and stop when they hear "purple light."
- **Simon Says Simon** This is a game to really make your students think twice! Ask for two "Simon" volunteers. Designate which "Simon" leader should be obeyed and which "Simon" leader will expect the backwards reactions (the opposite of what was called out).
- **Toe Tac Tic** If a student gets three Xs or Os in a row, she loses the game instead of winning in the traditional manner.
- **Double Duck Goose** Two people link arms and tap a person on the head. Both individuals must sit.

ICE TIP:
Often students learn more from what is not said a loud. The best teaching advice I know was from my pastor who reminds me to teach those around me and, only when completely necessary, to use words.

move it out!

PURPOSE:
This is a remixed version of "Sing It Out!" from **ICEBREAKERS: 60 FUN ACTIVITES THAT WILL BUILD A BETTER CHOIR!** This fast and fun adaptation is great for the beginning of school year, a retreat, or anytime your choir needs to get moving. This is a fantastic way to pair up students without having an individual picked last or not at all.

REQUIREMENTS:
One slip of paper for each student in the class
Container for the slips of paper

PREPARATION:
Predetermine a list of popular song titles that have recognizable dances (i.e. the Macarena or the Electric Slide). Print two copies of each of the titles on the slips of paper, so each person will have a match for his song. (40 students = 20 song titles)

DIRECTIONS:
1. Instruct students to make one large circle around the room. If there are more than 40 people in the circle, you may want to create multiple circles.
2. As you hand out the slips of paper, ask the students privately to study the title, without demonstrating the type of dance in the title or singing any of the lyrics.
3. Explain that the goal of this non-verbal icebreaker is to find the other person who has the matching song title/dance listed on his slip of paper. This is achieved by watching the dances of the other students in the circle. After several attempts, if a student is unable to find his match, he can then sing the first line of the song.
4. Start the game by saying "Ready, set, move!"
5. Inform the class that once a match is made, the two students sit, introduce themselves, and share three things about themselves (i.e. favorite musical style, performer, and band).
6. Once everyone has found his partner, allow the couple to stand and demonstrate the moves featured on their slips of paper. Let their classmates guess what song the moves represent. The pair can then introduce each other to the class.

VARIATION:
If the instructor wants to form smaller groups from the larger one, try making larger groups by using fewer song/dance titles. Instead of two people matched up with one song, consider dividing a 100-voice choir with ten songs to split the choir into ten equal groups (one song title per group).

ICE TIPS:
- This fun activity helps students with simple choreography as well as opening them up to not feel so inhibited with movement.
- A list of 50 song titles is provided in the back of the book.

folder scramble

IceBreakers 2: IceBreakers - Remixed!

PURPOSE:
Folder Scramble helps to prepare students for the physical movement that takes place in a music ensemble. Students share stands and folders, help each other with instruments, select dance partners, move equipment, build sets, share microphones, offer high-fives after a great rehearsal, and hugs after performing a well-deserved solo. This sly trick to prepare students to hold hands or work in close proximity with classmates really works. Students must rely on successful communication skills.

REQUIREMENTS:
A folder or piece of music for each participating student
Shoes, hats, notebooks, small backpacks, props, instrument cases (optional)
Plenty of space for the students to make two large circles

PREPARATION:
None

DIRECTIONS:
1. Ask students to make a circle of 10-20 people. If more than 20 students are participating, form multiple circles.
2. Explain that each student should clearly label her choral folder and a piece of music. If folders are not available, other items could be substituted, such as clothing, empty backpacks, and even small instrument cases.
3. Students place their folders in a pile in the center of the circle.
4. The participants step back into circle formation and grasp hands with students on either side.
5. At the starting signal, students must pick up their folder of music without letting go of the hands of the people on either side of them.
6. If students release their hands and the circle is broken, all items go back to the pile in the center and the game begins again.

VARIATION:
Friendly Team Folder Scramble All students put their belongings in the center of the room and then form two straight rows facing each other on either side of the belongings. The object of this game is to pick up the opposing team's music and hand it to them without letting go of their neighbors' hands in your own line. The two lines must stay in straight lines and continue holding hands. This variation ensures students get to know each other's names as they see the name on the folder and must make a delivery. This variation may present communication challenges.

ICE TIPS:
- Do NOT use any delicate items that could be damaged in the circle grab.
- Keep the icebreaker positive and avoid any potential conflicts.

PURPOSE:
Ba-da Bingo is the physical equivalent of bingo with a physical-fitness twist that will get your students' blood pumping! After just one round of **Ba-da Bingo**, your class should be too exhausted to do anything but sit down, pay attention, and listen.

REQUIREMENTS:
Bingo cards (one per student and the entire physical list for the Ba-da Bingo leader)
Writing utensils
Balloons, hula-hoops, music folder, yardsticks, toothpicks, and oranges (optional)

PREPARATION:
Create Ba-da Bingo cards with physical activities in each square on the grid. Brainstorm a list of 50 physical movements. Keeping the center square free, design a card with 24 squares, each containing a physical idea. Use the web for online teacher resources for ideas to create your own custom bingo card. Free printable blank cards are available from various websites.

DIRECTIONS:
1. Give each student a Ba-da Bingo card and a writing utensil.
2. Explain that students move around the room, looking for a fellow classmate to perform one of the physical activities on the card. When the activity is completed, that student writes her name in the appropriate square.
3. Once the entire card is filled (black-out style), the student yells "Ba-da bingo!" to be declared the winner.

VARIATIONS: Here are a few "physical" examples for the Ba-da Bingo card.
- Laugh a loud with another person for 15 seconds, holding tummy and rolling on the floor.
- Stand on one foot with one eye shut.
- Say "unique New York" eight times as fast as you can while jogging in place.
- Reach down and touch toes.
- Hula-hoop for 10 seconds with or without a hula-hoop.
- Balance a music folder on your head for 10 seconds.
- High-five and low-five a neighbor.
- Pass an orange without using any hands (from neck to neck).
- Demonstrate the proper way to make a hook shot with a pretend basketball.
- Do five backwards jumping jacks (feet together when hands go over head).
- Twist down to the ground and back up.
- Shake hands with your left hand on top, right hand on the bottom.
- Stand back to back and balance a yardstick on both partners' heads.
- Wink at a person without smiling.

The **"Blah" Faculty Variation** is a must for faculty in-service days. Use buzzwords from the in-service (i.e. assessment, rubric, and tech-anything) on the bingo card and when every space is full, the faculty member stands up and shouts, "Blah, blah, blah!" Not an icebreaker for the timid! ☺

ICE TIP:
Participants do not have to perform all activities on the Ba-da Bingo card. Each player just need to be able to execute one or two directives. Be creative!

flying fish

IceBreakers 2: IceBreakers - Remixed!

PURPOSE:
Flying Fish is a ridiculous game that encourages friendly competition. There are no hidden lessons here, just pure fun! Although messy, you'll find this activity provides great photo ops.

REQUIREMENTS:
One can of shaving cream or whipped topping
Two large boxes of Goldfish® crackers
Towels for clean up

PREPARATION:
Find an area with lots of room to spare (outdoors preferably)
Put towels under the "face" canvas
Choose "faces" without glasses or contacts (or fancy hairdos)

DIRECTIONS:
1. Divide the class into pairs. One person will be the canvas target and the other person will toss the flying fish. The canvas partner needs to stand with her hands behind her back.
2. Either you (or a responsible student volunteer) will apply shaving cream to the canvas partner's face.
3. The partner who will toss the fish collects a cup containing a predetermined number of goldfish crackers and takes three steps back from the target.
4. When the instructor announces, "On your mark, get set, FISH," the partner tosses the Goldfish® for 30 seconds trying to get the crackers to stick to the target. NOTE: Require the tossing partners to throw only one cracker at a time...do not throw "schools of fish."
5. At the end of 30 seconds, count how many fish stuck to the shaving cream on the face (or how many Goldfish® landed on the floor).
6. The winning team can claim to have the most crackers stuck to the target.

VARIATIONS:
- Use candy corn, colored cereal, or any other colorful and lightweight candy.
- Blindfold the person tossing the fish.
- Ask the target to lie down and the other person can toss fish from a closer distance.
- Cover hands with peanut butter. Toss puffed cereal at hands and see how many pieces of cereal stick. Before playing, confirm there are no peanut allergies.

ICE TIP:
- Remind the person getting his face filled with the shaving or whipped cream to keep his eyes closed and to remove glasses or contacts. It might be handy to use goggles for this icebreaker.
- There's nothing fishy about a student listening to instructions for her own safety!

PURPOSE:

Participants must keep their eyes on the conductor and the baton while performing this not-so simple exercise. The **On Your Mark** icebreaker simulates making music, rehearsing using peripheral vision. Each ensemble member needs to focus on the conductor, as well as the person standing next to her. It is easy to stumble if you are not hyper-focused on the goal (or the baton). The team is only as strong as the weakest link.

REQUIREMENTS:

A conductor with a baton
A "team baton" for each group (a water bottle, a shoe, or a choir folder can be substituted)
Space for two or more lines of students

PREPARATION:

None

DIRECTIONS:

1. Divide the class into two teams.
2. Teams form straight lines (elbow distance from each other).
3. The line leader at the front of the line holds the "student baton" for each team.
4. As the instructor begins conducting (with or without a baton) and the students begin to sing or play the designated piece, they start passing the student baton from the front of the line to the back.
5. To encourage students' attention during this activity, tell the students that when they see the music cut-off (unexpected cut-offs work best for this game), the musicians must sit on the floor.
6. The team that moves the baton farthest down the line wins that round. Note: The team loses a point if they have any wiggles or noise after the director's cut-off. In other words, it pays to watch the conductor's baton, as well as the people and action next to you.
7. If the conductor does not cut off the music and the team baton makes it all the way to the end, the last person in line must run to the front of the line and the team baton is passed back again. If there is a tie, whichever team sits down the fastest gets the point.

VARIATIONS:

- **Twirling Batons** To achieve additional physical activity, spread the students out so they are five-ten feet apart. After each student receives the baton, he has to spin around once.
- **Backwards ...Mark, You're On** For an added challenge, try moving backwards.

ICE TIPS:

- The "baton pass" works best as an obstacle free outside activity or inside a gymnasium.
- This is a great exercise teaching students to watch the conductor. Participants will get so involved in the game that they will forget to look up. (Sound familiar?) Even if the team baton makes it down the line first, if the team doesn't freeze at the conductor's cut-off, all effort is in vain. Students also develop teamwork skills as they must figure out how to pass the baton quickly.
- The smoother the passing technique, the farther the team will go.

leader of the pack

IceBreakers 2: IceBreakers - Remixed!

PURPOSE:
Even the smallest details make a big difference! Sometimes as music educators we look at the big picture and forget to focus on the "smaller stuff" so the "bigger stuff" will work. Our students would benefit from learning better observation and listening skills. Much of what we do as teachers must be caught and not taught.

REQUIREMENTS:
None

PREPARATION:
None

DIRECTIONS:
1. Instruct students to sit in a circle.
2. Choose a person to be the wolf. Ask the wolf to leave the room.
3. Choose a leader of the pack who will make small gestures without getting caught.
4. The wolf returns and stands in the middle of the circle, circling to identify the leader of the pack.
5. The leader of the pack should make small, discreet actions (anything from crossing or uncrossing legs, tilting or scratching the head, folding arms, snapping fingers, tapping toes, clasping hands, fixing hair, leaning in the chair, or looking right or left). The class immediately follows the action of leader of the pack as she switches to a new position or action. The objective is for the leader of the pack to be subtle in her actions so the wolf doesn't catch her, but obvious enough that the rest of the class members can imitate her actions quickly.
6. Once the leader of the pack is "caught" by the wolf, a new wolf is chosen and the second round of the game begins.

VARIATIONS:
- **Mirror Game** The students in the circle repeat the actions of the person in the middle of the circle – without being verbally instructed. Follow the leader move for move.
- **Echo Game** The students around the perimeter of the circle repeat the actions of the person in the middle. But there's a twist. The actions of the students in the circle's perimeter are delayed by four counts – thus the movement echo. Students execute the actions while watching the leader and having to think ahead. This lesson is good practice for performers who have to turn music pages or remember a sequence of dance steps.

ICE TIPS:
- Students can't go to sleep in this exercise or the wolf will win every time.
- Students learn to listen with their eyes as well as with their ears to catch the finer aspects in music and in life. For effective communication, a student must learn to listen actively and constructively.
- A good lesson for the choir is to imitate the conductor's posture, energy, and dynamics.

I C E B R E A K E R S

kiki's whoppit game

IceBreakers 2: IceBreakers - Remixed!

PURPOSE:
Kiki's Whoppit Game is one of my favorite games! The participants must learn names at a surprising rate or they'll get "whopped" with a rolled-up newspaper. Make sure your students can be trusted with rolled up newspapers (or squirt guns for the variation).

REQUIREMENTS:
None

PREPARATION:
One rolled up newspaper, a Nerf toy, or a swimming noodle
One squirt gun (for the variation)

DIRECTIONS:
1. Ask students to form circles of 10–20 people. If more than 20 participants, make multiple circles.
2. Give the first person who stands a rolled-up newspaper and instruct the Whoppit-eer to stand in the center of the circle.
3. To start the game, the instructor shouts out a student's name who is standing in the perimeter of the circle.
4. The person in the middle of circle attempts to identify that named person and lightly tap the person on the shoulder, arm, or chest.
5. The objective is before the "victim" is whopped, he must say another person's name who is also in the circle. If he gets hit before he can shout out the new person's name, he is declared the "whoppit-eer," taking the newspaper and moving into position in the center of the circle. The instructor shouts out a person's name and the game continues.

VARIATIONS:
- **Squirt Gun Name Game** Play this variation in the same manner as above outdoors, but the person is squirted if she cannot say another person's name in time.
- **Last (Or Middle) Name Whoppit Game** While this variation is played in the same manner, challenge your students by using last names, middle names, hometowns, or any other interesting trivia.

ICE TIPS:
- Make this activity more challenging by making the circle smaller with the participants standing shoulder-to-shoulder. If you want to move the students through the activity more often, call out the person who is standing directly in the front view of the "whoppit-eer." Chances are one can whop faster than the person can think.
- Amazingly, even if you know everyone's name backwards and forwards, nerves can get the best of a person when the pressure is on and the mind goes blank.
- This icebreaker is sure to be a "hit" with students and teachers alike.

Thanks to my middle school teacher-friend, Karen (Kiki) Sims, for sharing this fun activity!

abc art (already been chewed!)

IceBreakers 2: IceBreakers - Remixed!

PURPOSE:
Is gum chewing a problem in your classroom? Do you remind students continuously to remove their gum? Is it difficult to hear the music over the smacking of lips, chomping teeth, and popping noises? Are you starting to lose sight of your students because of large pink bubbles covering their faces? If so, this is the exercise for you and your students!

REQUIREMENTS:
Sticks of gum (at least one stick per student)
Poster board
Wet wipes or hand sanitizer

PREPARATION:
Cut large musical symbols out of the poster board. Present the symbols on a table at the entrance to the music room so students immediately see them. Place sticks of gum in a bowl at the entrance.

DIRECTIONS:
1. As students arrive to music class, inform students that they are welcome to chew the stick of gum provided for an allotted amount of time (one minute suggested).
2. At the end of the allotted time, each student will have the opportunity to stick their "ABC (already been chewed) Gum" on to the musical symbol of his choice to create a 3D piece of ABC art. Instruct them to affix their gum as a blob, instead of flattening it out.
3. Point out that each student may only touch his own ABC gum...if he touches anyone else's gum, the entire work of art is thrown into the trashcan. You can imagine the agitation from other students when the musical notation with their gum is discarded!
4. Automatically after adhering his gum into the ABC art, each student cleans his hands with wet wipes or hand sanitizer.

VARIATIONS:
- **ABC Section Race** Hold a contest between sections (boys against girls, brass versus woodwinds, or altos versus sopranos) for the most creative ABC art. Options are endless. Take note how many students and faculty visit your classroom to see the exhibits.
- **ABC Bulk vs. Beauty** Let students decide which is a more important objective: the sheer mass and volume of the art piece, or how creative and aesthetic the finished piece.
- **Gum Art** Issue each student two sticks of bubble gum, two toothpicks, and two index cards. The goal is for students to make the most creative art sculpture without using their hands. Display the hilarious results for other classes and parents. Invite judges to choose a first place winner.

ICE TIP:
When finished, display the ABC artwork around the room. Ask your school's art teacher for advice on framing, shellacking, positioning on the walls, etc. This can be a collaborative effort between departments.

PURPOSE:

Standing O puts a new twist on the simple games of "hot and cold" and "hide and seek." All students are involved as they learn and rehearse dynamics and tempo markings (i.e. pianissimo, fortissimo, crescendos, decrescendos, etc). In addition, they are improving their listening skills as well as aural proficiency expertise. This is also a great activity to teach the meaning and significance of a standing ovation.

REQUIREMENTS:

One item that can be easily hidden
A room or an outside space with lots of nooks and crannies

PREPARATION:

None

DIRECTIONS:

1. Ask for a volunteer to be the first seeker who steps out of the classroom.
2. The class collectively chooses an item and hides it in the classroom.
3. The seeker returns and stands in the center of the classroom.
4. The goal is for the seeker to locate the object quickly with the assistance of the class.
5. The helpers, who stay seated in their chairs, will indicate that the seeker is "cold" (far away from the object) by clapping low, slow, and pianissimo. As the seeker gets "warmer" (closer to the object's hiding place), the helpers clap higher, faster, and louder. As the seeker moves around the room, the speed and dynamics of the applause should change constantly. At the crucial discovery point, the helpers may show how hot or cold the seeker is to the object by lifting their bodies one or two inches off their chairs.
6. When the seeker touches the hidden object, the class gives a standing ovation!

VARIATIONS:

Synchronized Standing Os For a challenge, attempt two, three, and even four different seekers *simultaneously*. To make this challenge possible, each seeker must be aware which students of the class are applauding him or her. The seekers have to really listen and watch their teammates' body language to find their hidden object.
Silent Standing O This is performed with students sitting on the floor (far from the object) or standing on tiptoes with arms raised to the ceiling. No verbalization.

ICE TIP:

Your class, full of individuals with different backgrounds and experiences, becomes caring and active learners when working together for a common cause. Try this activity for one week, using a stopwatch to see if your students can improve their seeking time. This icebreaker will get your students focused and ready them for the day!

power extension

IceBreakers 2: Stress Busters – Solving Problems as a Team

PURPOSE:
Students create symbols with an extension cord and their ingenuity. The students must interact with each other positively in order to create a finished design for the team. Working together, a team can be revered as the most "powerful" in the department!

REQUIREMENTS:
Two (or more) 50-foot extension cords
Plenty of space to spread out two groups who are holding 50-foot extension cords

PREPARATION:
None

DIRECTIONS:
1. Divide the class into two groups that each form a large circle.
2. Give each group a large extension cord.
3. Instruct each person in the circle to keep both hands on the extension cord.
4. The students can move their hands on the extension cord, but they are not allowed to trade places with anyone or let go of the cord.
5. The objective is that both groups race to see which ensemble can form the called-out designs first. (Take digital photos to prove a group's design, as well as protect a teacher's decision).

IDEAS FOR EXTENDING POWER DESIGNS:
_ ▲ Triangle
_ ■ Square
_ ⬟ Pentagon
_ ★ Star
_ ✳ Flower
_ ♥ Heart
_ ♣ Christmas Tree
_ ☺ Smiley Face (exception: several students will have to release the extension cord to become the eyes and smile on the inside of the smiley face)
_ (?) Your own "Extended Power" design

VARIATIONS:
• **Musical Extension** Create musical symbols with the extension cord (treble clef, fermata, bass clef, half note, etc). Instead of calling out the symbols, allow the students to make their own decisions about which symbol to form, what it looks like, and how to create the musical symbol cooperatively.
• **Senseless Power** What happens if the students try to create a figure without looking? How can they communicate without talking? Is it easier if one person gives directions?

ICE TIP:
This activity should reinforce communication skills, creativity, and leadership ability. Most of all, tell your students to not sweat the small stuff and just enjoy!

top hat and cane

PURPOSE:

Students learn teamwork where one must lead and one must follow. In class, as well as in life, it rarely works to have two leaders and no followers. At the same time, how can success occur with just followers and no leader? Both positions must have respect for each other for a successful ensemble. This icebreaker also provides exercise in the middle of rehearsal.

REQUIREMENTS:

One cane (or dowel rod) per couple
One top hat (baseball cap or any type of hat) per couple

PREPARATION:

Clear a path for students to walk. This activity works best outdoors or in a gymnasium.

DIRECTIONS:

1. Pair up students. Determine which will be the leader (who will wear the top hat) and which of the pair is the follower.
2. Explain that the goal is to keep the cane between the two partners and not let it fall to the floor.
3. Instruct the partners to face one another. The leader puts the top hat on her head and then places the cane on the right side of her ribcage and her partner's left side of the ribcage.
4. The leader (the one wearing the top hat) discreetly determines the route the pair will travel around the room for two minutes without letting the cane drop to the floor.
5. After the allotted amount of time, the leader moves the top hat from her head to her partner's head while keeping the cane squeezed tightly between the pair. At this action, the other person becomes the leader for two minutes, directing the path of the pair around the room without dropping the cane.
6. If the cane is dropped, both people must sit down.
7. The winners are the students who are still standing at the end of the game with the cane squeezed between them.

VARIATIONS:

- If space is limited, allow one couple at a time to go while the rest of the class dictates the path the partners will follow.
- This icebreaker can be performed back to back or with a balloon.

ICE TIPS:

- Sometimes we expect leaders to know where we want to go or where we think they should go, when in fact they have other plans.
- Discuss what happens when the leader and follower don't communicate effectively. It is a losing situation if both partners don't pull their weight in a given situation.
- Successful leaders have a vision and know where they are headed. Another good tip is to learn your place; if told to follow, then follow! If appointed as a leader, put on the big hat and go for it!

patterns

IceBreakers 2: Stress Busters – Solving Problems as a Team

PURPOSE:
Relationships are important for any successful team. Memorization is a much needed skill. Progress is made step by step. This icebreaker teaches students that if they focus, they can improve.

REQUIREMENTS:
A beanbag, wadded up piece of paper, Nerf ball, sand-filled balloon, or any type of soft throwing apparatus for each group

PREPARATION:
None

DIRECTIONS:
1. Divide students into groups of 10-20 players and ask each group to sit in a circle.
2. Ask for a volunteer in each circle who will start the game.
3. Explain that the objective is to toss the beanbag back and forth within the circle to different people so each group member has a turn. The last person with the beanbag tosses it to the first person.
4. The students have a pattern that they must repeat. Can they repeat the same exact sequence as the first time? Time them to see how fast they repeat the pattern. If the beanbag is dropped, it must go back to the leader and the pattern is repeated from the beginning.
5. After the second round, ask the group to discuss ways they can improve their time. Allow the students to come up with a plan. Time them again to see if their plan worked.

VARIATIONS:
- **Reverse Patterns** Challenge the students to repeat the pattern backwards.
- **Unvoiced Patterns** Classmates can help their peers using only motions (no voices).
- **Patterns Squared** Add a second (different colored) beanbag into the sequence. Challenge the group's thinking by starting the beanbag halfway through the first pattern. Continue adding three or four beanbags so students must stay focused.
- **Double Patterns** Have two equal-numbered groups compete against each other.

ICE TIP:
Discussion Questions:
- ✓ What happened when students were aware they were timed?
- ✓ Did the clock make anyone nervous or did it improve performance?
- ✓ How does this activity directly relate to the music class?
- ✓ When a concert or a contest is nearing, does the group work faster and harder to prepare?
- ✓ How did each group memorize the various patterns?
- ✓ If the ensemble is preparing for competition, does rehearsal process change? Why?

PURPOSE:
Musical Digits is a "thinking" activity that is also lots of fun. Have an educational agenda. Without realizing it, your students will "accidentally" improve both their math and music skills. This game can be played anywhere, even at recess. Warning: this game is addictive. Play at your own risk!

REQUIREMENTS:
None

PREPARATION:
If necessary, write the below KEY of note values on the chalkboard

MUSICAL DIGITS KEY:
1 = quarter note   2 = half note   3 = dotted half   4 = whole   5 = rest (behind back)

DIRECTIONS:
1. Ask the class to divide into small groups of three-four people who will form a small circle.
2. The students place both hands behind their backs.
3. Explain that each finger represents a note value. For example, call out, "Quarter notes!" and the students in the group hold out both index fingers (each index finger equals one beat or a quarter note).
4. Determine the youngest in the circle. He touches his right index finger to one of his team member's index fingers. The person who was tagged with the index finger says, "Half-note" (one plus one equals two counts or a half note).
5. The tagged person can now choose to touch any of the fingers in the circle. When that player touches someone else's finger(s) in the circle, the person who was just tagged has to add up the amount and translate it into a total of musical counts.
6. The game continues until a person's hand is touched and the value is five beats. At that point, the tagged person must say "rest" and put that hand behind their back again. They can continue to play with just one hand.
7. It is a fun challenge when added finger amounts are over five. If the amount is five, you must say "rest" and place that hand behind your back. If the fingers add up to six, seven, eight, or nine, the tagged person must subtract five and give the new answer (the rhythmic value). For example, if a player is holding up three fingers and the person tags with four fingers, the tagged person must think seven minus five equals two beats or a half note. At this point, the tagged person raises two index fingers. The winner of the game still has fingers up at the end of the game.

VARIATION:
If an advanced class needs a more challenging game, change the answer key, using eighth notes, sixteenth notes, thirty-second notes, etc.

ICE TIP:
It may take a few tries before figuring out this icebreaker. Don't give up as it is loads of fun! This is a game that might have been played before hand held videogames. No batteries required.

Special thanks to Zane Mack for his help in creating this icebreaker activity!

score or no score

IceBreakers 2: Stress Busters – Solving Problems as a Team

PURPOSE:
Score or No Score is a variation of the popular TV game show, "Deal or No Deal." Instead of just one contestant, a musical team will work together to outsmart the "maestro" and win the ultimate grand prize (make it a good prize - hall pass for a day or teacher putting away folders for a week). This will be a game that students request to play over and over.

REQUIREMENTS:
20 music stands (or music folders that contain the note values)
Sheets of paper

PREPARATION:
Prepare one note value on each sheet of paper (quarter notes, eighth notes, half notes, whole notes, dotted quarter notes, and rests of all values). For longevity, laminate the musical notation paper so they can be reused each year. Tape each sheet of paper (with the musical notation) on 20 music stands. To add to the anticipation, place the paper with the note value in a black folder on the stand (it will take longer to open and create more suspense in the game). Set up the stands throughout the room.

DIRECTIONS:
1. Explain that **Score or No Score** is a variation of the popular TV game show, "Deal or No Deal." Instead of a banker, there is a "maestro" in this icebreaker and the numbered briefcases are music stands turned backwards with a musical value taped to each.
2. Divide the class into four groups. Three of the groups will compete, while the fourth group choosing the note values must decide if they want to answer, "Accept the score" or "No score."
3. In each round, each group collectively tries to get the note values to add up closest to the highest amount (teacher's choice).

VARIATIONS:
- **Pitch Or No Pitch** This is the same game, except this variation uses notes on the staff. The higher or lower the pitch (the most ledger lines), the more points awarded to each group.
- **Case Or No Case** Instrumental cases are used. When opened, a piece of paper is displayed with the name of an instrument of the orchestra. The higher (or lower) the range of the instrument, the more points a group is awarded.

ICE TIPS:
- The "maestro" could be a parent volunteer, a student teacher, an accompanist, or even the principal. The students by the stands must practice patience, as they have to wait to be called upon to open the folder with the note or rest values. They can also be involved in the game and should be able to answer what type of note, rest, or pitch is being presented.
- Let the class brainstorm ideas for a grand prize (the teacher has veto power and the final say). Even a Payday® candy bar could be a nice treat and keep the students eagerly studying note values.

"is a puzzlement"

PURPOSE:
In the music theater production of "The King and I," the King says to Anna, "Is a puzzlement!" This icebreaker is much more than just solving a puzzle. In the beginning, this stress-producing activity might not make sense and there might not be an apparent solution. Success will only be achieved when students realize they must work together as a team to solve the puzzles. It is necessary for each student to go outside his own group, clique, and comfort zone to achieve the team's goal.

REQUIREMENTS:
One 20-50 piece child's puzzle for each group (four to eight groups is best)
Floor space for each group for the puzzle pieces

PREPARATION:
Before the game begins and unbeknownst to the players, take out three or four puzzle pieces out of each box and switch the pieces with other boxes. For mystery-sake, present the pieces in a brown paper sack to each participating group.

DIRECTIONS:
1. Divide the class into four-eight small groups.
2. Give each group the sack of puzzle pieces. Note: Keep the secret of the switched puzzle pieces or the lesson will not work.
3. Explain that you will time each group to see how fast they can put the puzzle together. If group members ask for help, be evasive and encourage them to discover other resources that may be available.
4. After some confusion between the groups, share with them that all the puzzle pieces or parts of the melody were available at one time. Although you do not have them in your possession, all of the puzzle pieces were distributed. Suggest that this task can be accomplished with some creative problem-solving.
5. After the exercise, lead a discussion with some of these questions:
   a. Did cooperation take place or did competition take over?
   b. How beneficial is it to the team to reach out and ask for help?
   c. How long did this process take? Was there much wasted time?
   d. What kind of implications does this activity translate for your classroom?

VARIATION:
If you don't have puzzles available, create your own by using magazines, quotes with missing words, or a well-known piece of music (if you are not planning on reusing). Again, mix up the words or measures so students have to rely on each other to succeed.

ICE TIP:
People are diverse, but they each have answers and talents to share. It takes everyone's piece of the puzzle to complete the finished product successfully. Sometimes, the solution is found by thinking outside the box!

top ten arguments

IceBreakers 2: Stress Busters – Solving Problems as a Team

PURPOSE:
As an educator, sometimes you want to encourage healthy argument. Invite the principal, board member, and parents to hear the "arguments" about how important the subject is and all of the benefits they are receiving. This is a great activity to videotape and use for program recruitment.

REQUIREMENTS:
A sheet of paper and a writing utensil for each student
Writing board and markers
Handouts with Abraham Maslow's "Hierarchy of Needs" which can be found in Shawnee Press' *The Perfect Rehearsal* by Tim Seelig (a must-have for any choral conductor's library!)

PREPARATION:
Prepare handouts of Abraham Maslow's "Hierarchy of Needs" that include the following headers: biological, safety, attachment, esteem, cognitive, aesthetic, self-actualization, and spiritual.

DIRECTIONS:
1. Hand out the sheet with the "Hierarchy of Needs". Discuss how Maslow's theory of achieving basic human needs is covered by singing in a chorus. Here are some ideas:
   a. Biological: Musicians use oxygen. Many instructors or parent groups provide refreshments/treats to the groups after rehearsals or performances.
   b. Safety: The rehearsal room is a place of safety, respect, order, discipline, and trust.
   c. Attachment: Connection with the instructor, each other, and the audience.
   d. Esteem: Achievement, mastery, independence, pride in accomplishment.
   e. Cognitive: Studies show that creating music improves I.Q. Enough said!
   f. Aesthetic: Musicians are on a constant search for beauty. It is written that music is a gift so rare that it is shared by the angels in heaven. (Football is never mentioned!)
   g. Self-Actualization: The music student realizes her personal potential and seeks personal growth while striving for mountaintop experiences.
   h. Spiritual: Musicians grow spiritually and are encouraged to love and respect.
2. Ask each student to list top ten reasons a person should be involved in music.
3. Encourage each to reflect on why they are personally involved in music.
4. Pair up students to work together to agree on and then prioritize their top ten reasons.
   a. Continue combining groups. Each round, the groups must come to a consensus.
   b. By the end of the assignment, one large group must discuss, prioritize, and agree on the final top ten.

VARIATION:
Design a poster to remind your students what they believe and what music is doing for them personally. Each time they step into the rehearsal room, their beliefs are reinforced.

ICE TIP:
There are few activities that meet as many basic human needs as participating in a music class or a musical ensemble.

smash mouth

PURPOSE:

Smash Mouth is a challenging activity that requires cooperation (especially the variations). Allow the students to laugh and enjoy this silly game. When you learn to not take yourself and the situation so seriously, the solution may be right in front of you. Maybe there really is something to the message in Mary Poppins' song, "Just a Spoonful of Sugar".

REQUIREMENTS:

Two bags of mini-marshmallows (gummy worms, grapes, Jell-O, popcorn, whipped cream, potato chips, or small candies can be substituted)
Plastic spoons
Blindfolds
Wet wipes or hand sanitizer

PREPARATION:

Prepare the supplies.

DIRECTIONS:

1. Ask students to pair up into partners.
2. Explain that the blindfolded partner will attempt to pick up marshmallows with the plastic spoon and place them in the partner's mouth. The receiving student can give verbal directions, instructing the spoon-feeder where the marshmallows are located and guidelines on how to accomplish the task.
3. After ten marshmallows make it into the targeted mouth, the partners switch places and the eater now becomes the blindfolded feeder. Repeat the process.
4. The winning couple has each eaten ten mini-marshmallows and sat down first.

VARIATIONS:

- **Blind Smash Mouth** Both students are blindfolded.
- **Alternating Smash Mouth** Both students are blindfolded and alternate in feeding each other marshmallows. Supply plastic spoons to both students.
- **Circle Smash Mouth** Invite the class to make one large circle. At the instructor's directions, students place a marshmallow on their spoon and try simultaneously feeding it to the person on their left. This is a game for the fearless!

ICE TIP:

This icebreaker is easier if the partners slow down and take time to communicate. If your class finds that the spoons provide too much of a challenge, use plastic forks or clean hands.

marsh-ball

IceBreakers 2: Stress Busters – Solving Problems as a Team

PURPOSE:
Marsh-ball can be played inside or outside. Not nearly as painful as playing dodgeball, even if you are hit, the marshmallows won't leave a mark. The class will enjoy working as a team. As a teacher, they'll be "eating out of your hand" in no time!

REQUIREMENTS:
Several bags of large marshmallows
Masking tape or material to make a line to divide the classroom
Space for the students to move around

PREPARATION:
Place a line down the middle of the playing field. Mark boundaries.

DIRECTIONS:
1. The instructor numbers off the students (a sure-fire way to separate friends who stand next to each other).
2. The team members take their place behind the line and choose a name for the group.
3. Inform students that at the starting signal, they will place one hand behind their back and toss one marshmallow at a time at members of the other team.
4. If a student gets "marsh-balled" (a.k.a. nailed with a marshmallow), he must sit on the sidelines until allowed to re-enter the game.
5. If a marshmallow is caught, the person who threw the marshmallow is out. In addition, a team member of the catcher who was sitting on the sidelines can reenter the game.
6. The game concludes when everyone is on one team.
7. Discuss how this game pertains to the classroom dynamics?

VARIATIONS:
• **Senior's Last Day Of School Marsh-Ball** In honor of graduating students, allow them to play with the new rule that they can use both hands to toss and catch marshmallows. Make it more challenging by giving them certain target areas (legs, chest, feet, arms). Points will be deducted if they make contact with the non-target areas of the body.
• **Seated Marsh-Ball** Try using chairs, or sitting on the floor in this variation.
• **Rolling Marsh-Balls** Roll on tummy and back, but do not allow feet to touch the floor.

ICE TIP:
For competitive or aggressive students (or just to even the playing field), inform them that players can only throw with their weaker or non-dominant arm. If all else fails, blindfold the aggressive player. This should take care of the aggressiveness problem right away.

I C E B R E A K E R S

ping-pong pitch

PURPOSE:
Players are encouraged to set goals and improve them through a fast paced ping-pong ball-pitching game (you thought this was about a musical pitch, didn't you?). This icebreaker is most needed when ensemble members need to work on cooperation skills. This simple game reminds students to be patient with each member on the team.

REQUIREMENTS:
One ping-pong ball for each participant
Space to move around
An even amount of students to participate

PREPARATION:
None

DIRECTIONS:
1. Hand a ping-pong ball to each student.
2. Ask the students to form one large circle.
3. Count off the students. All of the odd numbered students step into the center of the circle and face the even numbered students. To ensure that each has a partner, instruct them to shake the facing partner's hand.
4. Tell students to toss their ping-pong ball into the air and attempt to catch it. Count how many are dropped each time. Repeat several times to improve dexterity.
5. Instruct the odd numbered students to walk in a clockwise circle as the even numbered students walk in a counterclockwise circle.
6. As the students walk, count off, "One, two, three, pitch!" When the students hear that cue, they stop walking and toss their ping-pong balls up in the air and catch it.
7. Analyze the icebreaker and what implications it can have in a classroom?

VARIATIONS:
- As the two circles of students walk in their designated direction, this time when they stop they will face a new partner. Immediately toss and catch the other person's ping-pong balls simultaneously. Track how many balls hit the floor.
- Use tennis balls, balloons, shoes, eggs, or water balloons (if outside). It may be a totally different kind of game!

ICE TIP:
As the class debriefs, explain that the ping-pong ball metaphorically represents a goal. When the student was just concerned about his or her own goals, there were not as many missed goals (dropped balls). The ball was easy to see and each student could easily accomplish one personal goal but the students may have struggled when they had to connect with a partner to achieve a mutual goal. What happens when the choir sets a group goal and works as an ensemble? With that collective goal, try the icebreaker again without dropping any ping pong balls. Did it work?

Thanks to my friend and colleague, Paul Gulsvig, for inspiring this activity.

balloon busters

IceBreakers 2: Stress Busters – Solving Problems as a Team

PURPOSE:
Balloon Busters involves highly charged activities that encourage student cooperation.

REQUIREMENTS:
Balloons
Space to move around
Music (optional)

PREPARATION:
None

DIRECTIONS:
1. Ask each student to tie a balloon around her ankle.
2. At the starting whistle, each student protects the balloon tied around her own ankle while trying to step on and burst other players' balloons.
3. The winner has the remaining inflated balloon tied to her ankle.

VARIATIONS:
- **Balloon Blast Off Race** Partners stand in a straight line with an inflated balloon that has not been tied. Can the pair figure out how to get the balloon across the room?
- **Balloon Throw Race** Partners throw a tied balloon as far as they can. Who wins?
- **Balloon Freeze** The class tries to keep a balloon in the air while feet stay frozen to the floor.
- **Balloon Siding** Partners stand back to back with a balloon lodged between them and turn their bodies to face one another (not dropping the balloon or using any hands).
- **Balloon Sliding** Play baseball with a balloon, each player using his own arm as the bat.
- **Balloon Spinning** Throw a balloon in the air. Partners spin 360 degrees and switch places before the balloon comes back down.
- **Balloon Dribbling Race** Students race down a preset course, dribbling the balloon up in the air. Partners must take turns and use every other hand to hit the balloon. If the balloon touches the floor, the pair must start over.
- **Balloon Sitting** Place a balloon on each chair. Who can pop their balloon first?
- **Hot Air Balloons** Give each student a balloon. Instruct students to lie on their backs. The winner keeps the balloon in the air (talk about good air support for musicians!).
- **Balloon Sculpture** Create a sculpture that represents and reflects the group's goals.
- **Balloon Blanks** Students brainstorm their own icebreaker with a fill-in-the-blank. Let each one (or in pairs) create a game using a balloon. Allow students the joy of creativity.
- **It's Electric!** Generate electricity by rubbing a balloon on clothes. Stick on wall.

ICE TIPS:
- Keep extra balloons on hand.
- Check with class to make sure there are no latex allergies.
- Warn neighboring classroom teachers of the possible raised noise level. Better yet, invite their classes to join in the fun!

ice cubes and chopsticks

26

IceBreakers 2: Creative Activities – Thinking Outside the Box

PURPOSE:
Teamwork!

REQUIREMENTS:
Ice cubes (or marshmallows)
A pair of chopsticks for each relay team
A plastic or paper plate for each relay team
Marshmallows or wadded up pieces of paper (variation)

PREPARATION:
Prepare a walking path between containers. Cool the room if using ice cubes for this icebreaker.

DIRECTIONS:
1. Place several ice cubes on each plate.
2. Split the class into relay teams. Half of the team members line up behind one plate. The remaining team members cross the room to stand behind the opposing plate.
3. At the starting signal, the first racer uses chopsticks to pick up an ice cube and carry it across the room to the opposing team's plate.
4. When the first racer reaches the opposing plate, she hands the chopsticks off to the first person in that line. He has the challenge of picking up the same ice cube and returning it to the starting position. The game continues with the next person in line.

VARIATIONS:
- **Left-handed Chopsticks** Notice what happens when asked to not use the dominant hand. The feeling the student experiences is the feeling that many left-handers deal with everyday in what they consider a "right-handed world." Let this variation remind us to be sensitive to those who have different proficiencies.
- **Elementary Chopsticks** Use marshmallows or wadded paper balls for younger children. The larger elements that aren't quite so slippery will help them to gain control of a challenging pair of chopsticks.
- **Extended Chopsticks** Raise hands above head as you pass the ice cubes. Lower arms when you reach your partner.
- **Getting to Know You Chopsticks** As each person is handed the pair of chopsticks, he must answer one of "Headliner" questions (found page 52 of the original *IceBreakers* book).

ICE TIPS:
- Ask for a volunteer to demonstrate the proper way to hold and to use chopsticks. Let that student have his time in the sun and share his skill with the rest of the class.
- Avoid using ice cubes in warm temperatures. For those warm weather climates, use marshmallows or paper formed into a ball.

topsy turvy

IceBreakers 2: Creative Activities – Thinking Outside the Box

PURPOSE:
Topsy Turvy is an icebreaker that takes total teamwork of every team members' ten toes! If the tablecloth falls to the ground, the team simply starts over, working together until they get it right. If at first you don't succeed, do it until it's right!

REQUIREMENTS:
One plastic tablecloth with a flannel backside
Large beach towel (variation)

PREPARATION:
None

DIRECTIONS:
1. Determine a space large enough so groups of students (4-20) can lay on backs in a large circle, pointing toes into the center of the circle. Although taking off shoes is not required, bare feet may be helpful to control the direction of the tablecloth.
2. Explain that on the count of three, students lift legs at a 45 degree angle.
3. Place one large plastic tablecloth on top of the students' feet that is perpendicular in the air (flannel side should touch everyone's feet).
4. Inform the participants that the number one rule is they can only use toes to do the work of moving the tablecloth...no one is allowed to touch the tablecloth with their hands.
5. Tell the students that this is not a win-lose game, but an icebreaker to build teamwork skills. So if the tablecloth falls to the floor, simply pick it up and place it back into starting position.
6. Challenge them to turn the tablecloth from the flannel-side down to the flannel-side up.

VARIATIONS:
- **Team Topsy Turvy** Several groups compete to turn the tablecloth over. Several tablecloths are required for this variation.
- **Triple Topsy Turvy** Stack three colored tablecloths on top of each other. Challenge the players to restack the tablecloths in any order without using their hands.
- **Twisted Topsy Turvy** Put your shoes or your socks on your hands and position your fists in the air. The objective is to use the shoes (on your hands) to turn the tablecloth.
- **Timed Topsy Turvy** Time the activity. Can the students beat their old time?
- **Total Topsy Turvy** Combine variations to totally challenge participants.

ICE TIPS:
- Warn students ahead of time that they should wear jeans or pants for this activity.
- If playing the activity outside, provide a blanket or tarp for the students to lie down on.

human machines

PURPOSE:
Like the character, Tevye in "Fiddler on the Roof," teachers can get so wrapped up in "traditions" that we forget that change can be good for us and even essential for personal growth. Use **Human Machines** to demonstrate how a "product" can be improved and turn out even better than before. Dare students to walk the road less traveled.

REQUIREMENTS:
Slips of paper

PREPARATION:
On each slip of paper, list a machine (i.e. kitchen appliances, car wash, washing machine, computer, popcorn popper, dishwasher, GPS system, soda fountain, assembly line, printing press, cotton gin, toaster, can opener, sprinkler system, stapler, pencil sharpener, iPod, cell phone, copy machine).

DIRECTIONS:
1. Divide the class into groups of 5-15 students.
2. Issue each group a slip of paper with the "machine" idea and inform the group that they must collectively act it out. The only rule is that each person in the group must be physically involved in the machine's operation. If students are itching to be creative, allow them to invent their own machine.
3. Give the students a time limit to discuss their presentation.
4. Watch as each "human machine" group performs for the rest of the class.
5. Time it! Determine the winning group by how quickly the other groups guessed correctly.

VARIATIONS:
- **Honkin' Human Machines** Add sound effects for added hilarity.
- **All-In-One Machine** Ask the entire class to combine to create one massive "Human Machine."
- **Reinventing the Human Wheel** The class cooperatively thinks of a good idea and creates a new machine with humans.
- **Human Machines + Props** Add handkerchiefs, ping-pong balls, plastic plates, dowel rods, notebooks, sticky notes, trashcan lids, brooms, balloons, and whatever else you find in the classroom to use as a prop.

ICE TIPS:
- Add music. Create a car wash machine while listening to the 1970s radio hit, *Car Wash* (by Rose Royce). The middle section of the song, "Work and Work" lends itself to choreography. Add cleaning rags for props and you've got a great routine – ready for performance! Let students know that they will receive extra credit for sound effects and use of props.
- The only constant in life is change.
- Change can present opportunities for improvement and advancement.

what comes after ti?

IceBreakers 2: Creative Activities – Thinking Outside the Box

PURPOSE:

What Comes After Ti? challenges your students' critical thinking skills by encouraging them to think outside the box. Because some aspects of our society are finite, people generally accept what we already know and what is most familiar. If time allows, research some of the musical scales and different sounds from around the world.

REQUIREMENTS:
None

PREPARATION:
None

DIRECTIONS:
1. Divide into teams of 3-8 players.
2. Explain that each team will invent a new note and a symbol for that note. This note or sound should be one that they haven't previously used (at least knowingly). ☺
3. The note and symbol should be found between any of the Solfège pitches and hand symbols (for example, find a note between Do and Di or between C and C#).
4. If your class does not use Solfège, try creating an alphabet letter. After A,B,C,D,E,F,G…what would come next (and it can't be "H" through "Z"). Invent a letter, sound, and hand symbol to describe that "new" note.

VARIATION:
Advanced classes can discuss when they might hear that new sound in a piece of music. Could the sound they heard be performed purposefully? A trombone sliding to a note, a violin's glissando, or a singer's portamento could all potentially have some of those quarter steps contained in those pitches.

ICE TIP:
While in some aspects of life, it may be ok to be a bit "off," this is not acceptable for musicians. If a musician is not 100% accurate, a little bit can make a big difference and the sound results into something other than what was written.

This is an email I received from one of my former students. This is why we should strive for perfection:

IF 99.9% IS GOOD ENOUGH, THEN…
- 2.5 million books will be shipped with the wrong covers.
- 268,500 defective tires will be shipped this year.
- 22,000 checks will be deducted from the wrong bank in the next 60 minutes.
- 20,000 incorrect drug prescriptions will be written this year.
- 1,314 phone calls will be misplaced by telecommunication services every minute.
- 114,500 mismatched pairs of shoes will be shipped this year.
- 291 pacemaker operations will be performed incorrectly.
- 18,322 pieces of mail will be mishandled each hour.
- 12 newborns will be given to the wrong parents daily.

Above my rehearsal door is the quote, "Perfect practice makes perfect performance." Even if complete perfection is unattainable, we should strive for excellence in all we do.

PURPOSE:
The Same Name Fame Game helps introduce students to one another by collecting information in an allotted amount of time. Classmates get a chance to find similarities as well as to reach an agreement on a given topic. Upon completion of this activity, students will have shared one-on-one time with several classmates in just a manner of minutes.

REQUIREMENTS:
One piece of notebook paper for each student
A writing utensil for each student
Chalkboard or dry erase board and markers

PREPARATION:
Post the following chart on a chalkboard:

NAME	SAME	FAME
1.		
2.		
3.		
4.		
5.		

DIRECTIONS:
1. Give each student a piece of paper and a writing utensil.
2. At the signal, each student sits facing a partner.
3. Inform the students of the 45-second process.
   a. On their piece of paper, write their partner's name on the first line in the first column (learning to spell their partner's name by seeing it in print, a great mnemonic device for learning names).
   b. The pairs must agree on one thing that the two have in common (i.e. both watch reality TV, both dislike cats, both are anchovy-lovers). Once an agreement is reached, they write what they have in common under "SAME."
   c. Under "FAME," the pair agrees on a "famous" person that the two would like to meet or what living famous person they would like to emulate?
4. Signal the time is up by blowing a whistle or playing an instrument to signify to find a new partner. The new partners must think of new material to share and can not repeat any similarities or famous people they admire.

VARIATIONS:
- Add the word, "AIM," into the key words. What do the two students "aim" to achieve in the ensemble as a goal one month or one year down the road?
- Use this activity throughout the year and change the key words. Determine which words would help you gain the most meaningful information about your students.

ICE TIP:
With the 45-second time limit, students will feel the urgency and know they should be movers and shakers (no slackers allowed). It also gives each student a chance to make several connections in a short amount of time.

initial that

IceBreakers 2: Creative Activities – Thinking Outside the Box

PURPOSE:
Initial That is a written project teaching problem-solving. The hidden benefit in this icebreaker is that you can find out students' concerns and their proposed solutions at the same time.

REQUIREMENTS:
One sheet of paper for each student
Writing utensils

PREPARATION:
None

DIRECTIONS:
1. Ask the students to sit on a circle on the floor or move their desks to a circle formation.
2. Explain that this icebreaker will give everyone a chance to list a concern and then allow other students to offer solutions. The students should be aware that the teacher will read the papers.
3. After giving students a piece of paper and writing utensil, ask them to think about and write down a one-line concern they have for the ensemble, the program, or even for themselves. On the off chance there are no concerns, they should write a concern that might arise in the coming weeks, months, or years.
4. Encourage the students to stay positive. This is not an invitation to air dirty laundry and individual names or places should not be mentioned. Hopefully, they will embrace this icebreaker as an important opportunity to better the department, the program, and themselves.
5. After each student writes down one concern, collect the papers, shuffle them, and pass them out to other classmates.
6. Each student has 30 seconds to silently read the concern and offer a solution or words of encouragement. Responses need to be one positive word or a short sentence.
7. Repeat the steps for several rounds.
8. All papers must be collected so you can read through each and decide how to best use the information.

VARIATION:
For more confidentiality, collect the concerns and type out the top ten noted concerns. Divide the class into groups that will work together to discuss solutions. This may be more work, but you retain control and the answers remain private.

ICE TIP:
Students can be a wonderful resource for solutions. Initially, students may be slow to voice concerns, but when voices are heard and ideas utilized, participation will follow. This is an opportunity for some "Dear Abby" advice – for your students, from your students.

PURPOSE:
Can you say SUPERCALIFRAGILISTICEXPIALIDOCIOUS backwards? People learn and memorize in completely different ways! This fun icebreaker can be done with small groups or individually. Not only good for the classroom, but a great trick for family gatherings, bus trips, or conversation starters.

REQUIREMENTS:
Write out SUOICODILAIPXECITSILIGARFILACREPUS on index cards or on marker board. (SUPERCALIFRAGILISTICEXPIALIDOCIOUS backwards)

PREPARATION:
None

DIRECTIONS:
1. Ask the class to recite "SUPERCALIFRAGILISTICEXPIALIDOCIOUS" aloud several times.
2. Pass out the cards with the backwards word to each student or each small group.
3. Ask the class to read the new word aloud slowly on their card several times, "SUOICODILAIPXECITSILIGARFILACREPUS."
4. Tell the students they have three minutes to memorize that phrase. (Do not give any further instructions, just say, "Begin!")
5. After three minutes, most students will be frustrated and haven't memorized the phrase.
6. Discuss memorization techniques. Let the students share how they each learn, giving them ownership of this activity, as well as providing useful hints for memorization. (Popular answers may include writing the phrase, reciting it over and over, putting it to music, adding movement, or breaking it into smaller patterns).
7. With these hints, give the groups a few more minutes to try the memorization systems discussed.
8. This time, ask the whole class, the small groups, or individuals to recite the phrase. Chances are good that they will be successful!

VARIATIONS:
- **Z, Y, X, W, and**... Recite the alphabet backwards
- **Spelling Supercalifrag**... The students form letters with their bodies (as in the Broadway production of "Mary Poppins.") This is a fun exercise that has a physical benefit as well!
- **Row, Row Syllable Style** Sing the nursery rhyme, "Row, row, row your boat." Keeping the rhythm, melody, and the words the same, take out the first word of the phrase, changing the syllabic emphasis. (Students will now sing "Row, row, your, boat gent.... Ly down the stream mer-lly, mer-illy, mer-illy, mer-illy, life is but a dream, row.")

ICE TIP:
People have a variety of learning styles: visual, auditory, tactile/kinesthetic, or multiple intelligences. Watch your students in this exercise and discover much about each of their learning styles.

crayon box

IceBreakers 2: Creative Activities – Thinking Outside the Box

PURPOSE:
Isn't it interesting that musicians can change their performance when focusing on a concept – including color. Children are like crayons – each one adding their own stamp of uniqueness to the class or ensemble. When making a piece of art, you need all of the colors for a resulting masterpiece. Too much or too little of a color can detract from the final piece.

REQUIREMENTS:
Box of crayons or colored pieces of paper
Paper and writing utensils

PREPARATION:
None

DIRECTIONS:
1. Explain to the class that as you hold up individual crayons, they should reflect how each color makes them feel and list a one-word adjective on their sheet of paper. Try 5-6 colors (red, yellow, black, white, blue, green, and orange).
2. Understandably, the students will have different personal interpretations of the colors.
3. Transfer the concept to playing an instrument or singing a section of a song. As you direct, instruct your ensemble to think of a specific color while performing.
4. Videotape this icebreaker exercise and allow the students to determine if they hear any difference in the performance when they were interpreting different colors (they should hear a difference in timbre if they listen closely).
5. Not only are they listening to what they played, this is a good way to study and listen to examples which will help memory work, listening skills, and analysis.
6. Discuss how people sing in color or think in color. What color do you think represents a happy sound? Sadness? Anger? Creativity? Intelligence? Love? Excitement?
7. Give each student a chance to offer their favorite color.

VARIATIONs:
- **Sing a Rainbow** Use stage lighting to create different moods for your singers and your audience. Imagine the impact of various colors of light or darkness flooding the stage.
- **Wear a Rainbow** Color can enhance costume changes on stage. Try adding colored scarves, white gloves, black hats, etc. to spice up the visual impact!
- **Taste a Rainbow** Provide a taste test of different colored jelly beans. Too easy to predict? Combine flavors and colors.

ICE TIPS:
- Technical people backstage are important. As teachers, we might pay little detail to the lighting of the shows, backdrops, costume colors, house lights, pre-show lighting, decorations, lobby decorations, program colors, and so on. You can affect the audience and the students' perceptions through simple effects in the auditorium, gym, or on stage.
- What memories do you have as a young child when you open a box of crayons? Studies have shown that the crayon scent can be therapeutic for people of all ages. Bring back that joy!

musical trip

PURPOSE:
Have you ever played the alphabet game of "I'm going on a trip and in my suitcase, I will pack...?" Traditionally the player answers with something that starts with the letter "A," like apple. Our **Musical Trip** requires students to utilize musical words and thoughts.

REQUIREMENTS:
None

PREPARATION:
Create a music words cheat sheet for each of the letters in the alphabet.

DIRECTIONS:
1. Start the game by saying, "I am going on music tour and I'll bring..." and fill in the blank with a musical word that starts with the letter "A."
2. The next student repeats, "I am going on music tour and I'll bring an _____ (insert an "A" word) and he adds a musical word that begins with the letter "B."
3. The game continues until you reach the letter "Z" (yes...there are Z musical words!).
4. To ensure students will be thinking of musical words for every letter, randomly select players in the circle.

VARIATIONS:
- **Composer Tour** "I'm going on tour and the composer I'll take is ..." Repeat the game using only composers' names. It may be necessary to use first, last, or even middle names.
- **Ear Training Expedition** Ask the first person to sing a note on "la." The next person sings the first person's note and adds a note. Continue as long as students can repeat the melody. It must be a new melody and not a recognizable tune.

ICE TIP:
Not only are students improving memory skills, but are also creatively coming up with musical words phrases, composers, etc. What other musical categories can the class list?

A: A-flat, andante, allegro, alto, arts
B: bass clef, baritone, ballet, bongos, blues, baton
C: classical, cello, crescendo, cymbals, clarinet
D: drums, dotted half, decrescendo, duet
E: electric guitars, eighth note, euphonium, encore
F: forte, fortissimo, flat, fermata, five chord, fifth
G: G-clef, glockenspiel, glissando, guitar
H: horn, harmonica, harmony, half note, hip-hop
I: instrument, interlude, impromptu
J: jingle bells, jazz, jammin'
K: kazoo, KISS (the band), key, key signature
L: legato, listen, Latino, lullaby

M: mezzo forte, melody, metal
N: note, natural, nocturne, neo-classical
O: octave, opera, obbligato, overture
P: piano, pianissimo, pop, pizzicato
Q: quarter note, quartet, quintet
R: reggae, rest, rock, rap, R&B, recital, rehearsal
S: snare, staff, staccato, symphony, soul, sing
T: treble clef, trumpet, timpani, trill, tonic, trio
U: ukulele, unison, ultra-loud
V: violin, vibrate, viola, vibrato, vivace
W: whole note, western, waltz
X: xylophone, x-tra rehearsal!
Y: yodeling, "yes I can"
Z: Zorba, zither

Thanks goes to my Music Theatre of Wichita friends, a group of 8-12 year-olds who compiled this list: Chandler Moore, Johanna Pfaff, Stevie Mack, Cassie Dalley, Abbey Dalley, Maria Collins, and Justin Kim.

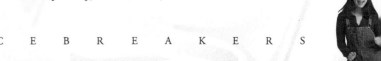

house of cards

IceBreakers 2: Creative Activities – Thinking Outside the Box

PURPOSE:
Teachers normally don't allow students' electronics into the classroom. Teaching is difficult when phones are ringing, fingers are texting, and students are listening to iPods or "facebooking." Here is an icebreaker when students can use cell phones in class.

REQUIREMENTS:
One deck of cards for each group
Masking tape for each group
One cell phone with photo and texting capabilities for each group
Tables, desks, or a flat space to build a house of cards
One tape measure

PREPARATION:
None

DIRECTIONS:
1. Divide students into groups of 4-6 people. Issue each group a deck of cards and a roll of masking tape.
2. Ask the students if they have ever built a house of cards. Ask the group to predict the size of their assembled house of cards and write down the guesstimate.
3. At the signal, each group will have ten minutes to construct a house of cards, measure, and name the structure. During that time, they can use their cell phones to text other people for ideas for the creation design and ask for guesses for the height of the building. Record these estimates as well.
4. Each group uses the cell phone to take a photo and send it to a friend outside the school who can name the creation. Award extra points to get a response from someone out-of-state and triple points if someone responds from outside the country.
5. The instructor measures each of the groups' houses with a measuring tape. Review the groups' estimates and also the incoming texts about the size and names suggested for the creation.
6. Award prizes for the tallest, the widest, the most creative, and the best name. If it is important for everyone to "be a winner" in your classroom, determine more categories (sturdiest foundation, funniest, scariest, fastest built, and slowest construction).

VARIATIONS:
• **House of Music** While considering safety, use instrument cases, folders, stands, sheet music, and any musical items to create a structure.
• **Anatomy House** Bodies are used to create a human pyramid or formation.

ICE TIP:
Observe the teamwork exhibited. Did one "engineer" emerge or did everyone plan and build?

PURPOSE:
Cultivate listening skills.

REQUIREMENTS:
Pennies dated before 1982 and pennies dated after 1983
Nickels, dimes, quarters, coin dollars
A hard floor, a wooden desk, or any surface that is not carpeted

PREPARATION:
None

DIRECTIONS:
1. Ask the students to shut their eyes during a musical demonstration.
2. Choose six students to approach the front of the room and hand each a coin (be sure you have at least one penny from before 1982 and one dated after 1983).
3. Starting with the highest-valued coin, cue each student to drop her coin on the floor.
4. Ask the rest of the class to vote by raising their hands showing which kind of coin they think was dropped. Students with above average listening skills will be able to distinguish which coins they heard, but the two pennies with different dates may cause some confusion.
5. Discussion: If given a listening test, could most students hear the difference in the timbre of the coins when they hit the flat surface? Ask a student to use musical words and phrases to explain the differences of tone color or timbre of each coin.

VARIATIONS:
Dollar Daze Partner students and give each pair a one dollar bill. The first person studies the front side and then asks his partner five questions about the front of the bill. They switch and the other player asks five questions about the back of the bill. Track correct answers. Was it easier to answer questions about the front or the back of the dollar bill? People handle money all the time, so why do we not pay attention to the obvious? Can this icebreaker translate to what details are being missed in rehearsal? Do we look intently or are we in a daze?

> **Dollar Daze** *Possible Questions: Where is George Washington looking? What three words are printed closest to the top of the bill? How many arrows is the eagle clutching in its talon? How many times does it say, "In God We Trust" on the front? On the back? Which way does the eagle's head turn? How many times is the number 1 spelled out "one"?*

ICE TIPS:
- After the class has tried this activity a few times, share the secret of the pennies. The newer pennies contain zinc, as well as copper, which is the reason for the duller sound when they hit the floor.
- Historians are not sure who "coined" the phrase, "a penny for your thoughts," but with the vast amount of multitasking teachers do these days, music educators are worth every pretty penny! Music educators have to be cent-sational listeners in more ways than one.

can you hear me now?

IceBreakers 2: Retreat Makers – Building Relationships

PURPOSE:
Can You Hear Me Now is filled with silliness and fun. Miscommunication can sometimes be comical in our daily lives, but gossip or half-truths can be hurtful. My mantra is to say about 10% of what you are thinking and you will be better off in life!

REQUIREMENTS:
None

PREPARATION:
None

DIRECTIONS:
1. Students sit in a tight circle on the floor (close enough to whisper into each other's ears).
2. The cell phone leader whispers a phrase to the person seated on her right and immediately after, she whispers the same phrase to the person seated on her left.
3. Similar to the childhood game of "Gossip" or "Telephone," the phrase travels both directions around the circle. When the phrase has worked its way back to the leader, the people on either side of her announce the statement. Even though the phrase started out the same, did it end the same going through many people?
4. To make the game more exciting add sound effects like cell phone static (for example, a "k-k-k-k" sound might be heard on a cell phone that is not getting good reception). Each student has to decipher what the message was without repeating the static noise. While students can add the static (within reason) to the phrase as it travels around the circle, the final people should say it clearly as the final message.

VARIATIONS:
- **Can You See Me Now?** Each person needs a piece of paper and a writing utensil. The leader draws a simple picture and shows it only to the person on her right. No one else is allowed to see the drawing. That second person now repeats the drawing, trying to sketch what the leader depicted on his page. In conclusion, compare the first drawing with the last piece of art. Were they similar? What changes were made?
- **Funny Face Shared** The leader holds his hands up to block his face and turns to his left, making a funny face (sticking out tongue, winking, making fish lips) that can only be seen by the person on his left. One by one the face is secretly passed down the line. Finally, contrast the last face with the first face made by the leader. How different are they?
- **Two-faced Circle** Leader sends a funny face in one direction of the circle and a different face the other direction in the circle. The person who receives both faces simultaneously stages a dramatic death.
- **Face the Music** Add various styles of music. The face must match the musical theme.

ICE TIP:
Food for thought: It is noted that while people are on the telephone, they hear 20% of what was actually said, but 80% of the communication was due to the tone of the voice. What tone do you share with others?

label fable

PURPOSE:
How often do we label people before really getting to know them? Many times that label just isn't fair or deserved. This icebreaker will give you an idea of how it feels to be "mislabeled."

REQUIREMENTS:
Nametags or masking tape with one word statements

PREPARATION:
Write a short statement on each of the nametags. Here are some statements you may consider:

Respect me.	Ignore me.	Roll your eyes at me.
Agree with me.	Interrupt me.	Be disinterested.
Believe in me.	Argue with me.	Make someone else a leader.
Show your passion.	Be disrespectful.	Text on your phone when I talk.
Value what I have to say.	Laugh at all I say.	Don't look in my eyes.

DIRECTIONS:
1. As students arrive, stick a nametag on each student's forehead or back. The student must not know what their nametag says.
2. Give groups an assignment or a task to problem-solve.
3. The groups should work quietly together, reacting to each other in the manner that the nametags suggest.
4. After five minutes, stop the activity and lead a discussion about how the exercise made each person feel. What was their reaction? How do we label classmates and people that we don't know? Is that fair? Have your students experienced treatment like that before? How can we change our stereotyping habits? How can we invite others to treat us fairly?

VARIATIONS:
- Split the class into two sections, one group with labels while the second group observes and takes notes.
- Create new labels to fit your classroom situation.
- Let students brainstorm new statements and see how the actions play out.

ICE TIPS:
- Discuss a time when you were mislabeled or stereotyped. How did that make you feel? What are some ways we can build relationships and respect each other, both verbally and non-verbally?
- Research shows that over half of the effect of a message depends on body language. Hiding hands can suggest a person feels insecure while folding arms may indicate he is not interested and palms down can signify that person is not telling the truth.

"to be or not to be?"

IceBreakers 2: Retreat Makers – Building Relationships

PURPOSE:
"To Be or Not To Be?" That is just one of the questions in this silly, imaginative, and noncompetitive game that will develop positive social orientation, expand creativity skills, stretch a body physically, and increase kinesthetic intelligence. Most importantly, students will learn stage directions and theater terms while moving in the "right" direction!

REQUIREMENTS:
One large space to play (cleared of shoes, books, or other items)

PREPARATION:
List of stage directions: stage right, stage left, center stage, down stage, up stage (Combine directions for more fun: Upstage left, down center stage, the pit, the house, the proscenium)

DIRECTIONS:
1. Ask students to stand and move to the designated "play area."
2. For a challenge, do not offer tips the first time the class plays the game. This icebreaker will help you to discover how much stage experience or terminology each student possesses without quizzing each personally.
3. Tell students they will walk briskly to areas of the stage as you shout out stage terms or directions. Each group must move together and no one can be left out of the mob.
4. While students may not know stage directions right away, by repeating this activity, students will catch on and make less and less mistakes on stage.

VARIATIONS OF STAGE DIRECTIONS:
- **The Director Is Coming** On cue, students form straight lines and fold hands in an opera pose, or band members must pretend to sit in a chair with instrument ready.
- **The Choreographer Is Near** Separate students into small groups. On cue, students freeze in a ridiculous group pose with each person in the group physically connected.
- **Rock Band** On cue, students must play an air instrument and jam.
- **Dance It Out** Shout out styles of dance or music (jazz, tap, hip-hop, country, ballet) and students dance in that style until the next term is called.
- **Scary Stage Mom** On cue, students give threatening looks and shake their index finger.
- **Audience In the House** Everyone must quickly sit down on the floor and start applauding.
- **Diva Moment** Act like a drama queen, fixing hair and vocalizing in a pretend microphone.

ICE TIP:
Let students have a hand at creating more variations to this game. Take turns where smaller groups compete against each other. Which group of students can quickly follow instructions and know where they are going on stage? Be sure none of the students are "left out" in this activity.

PURPOSE:
Perfect for retreats! The tapestry created represents the ensemble or class members' importance in all functions, performances, and rehearsals. When one person slides her yarn off the stake, it jeopardizes the final result.

REQUIREMENTS:
One huge ball of multicolored yarn
One 18" wooden dowel rod for each student

PREPARATION:
Cut the yarn into many different lengths. Tie the yarn lengths together and wrap into one large ball. Sharpen one end of each dowel rod so the students can easily spear the rod into the ground.

DIRECTIONS:
1. Invite students to sit in a circle and pound dowels into the ground in front of each individual.
2. The leader begins the activity by tying the yarn to his stake. He instructs each student that when they receive the yarn, they should share one personal or group goal he would like to achieve.
3. Throw the ball of yarn to a person sitting across the circle who will wrap the yarn tightly around her dowel rod and share a goal with the group. She will throw the yarn to the next catcher.
4. Keep tossing the yarn until all students have had a turn and have shared goals about themselves or the ensemble.
5. After everyone has had a turn, ask the students to look at the tapestry and discuss how each person in the group is connected as a whole through different avenues. Like the tapestry, your chorus is tightly bound. When one person feels happiness, joy, or sorrow, the group shares those feelings. Consider the end result when all members work together.
6. Finally, ask one student to slide their yarn off their stake. Notice what happens when one person fails to live up to their agreement or fails to communicate. Failure by one member will affect the entire group and can destroy all the good that has been done up to that point. It just takes one person to ruin the tapestry. The group functions best as a whole and success takes everyone's cooperation and positive attitudes.

VARIATION:
Instead of a personal or group goal, the participants can share what they believe they contribute to the ensemble or what talent they add to the picture.

ICE TIPS:
- Save the tapestry and hang it on the classroom wall as a reminder of the different friends, talents, and personalities that all came together to form one musical masterpiece during a special retreat.
- This activity is best played outside at a retreat so you can put the dowel rods into the ground. If that is not an option, the students can hold on to them to stabilize the rods.
- If outdoors, long slender sticks or small tree branches will work instead of dowel rods.

simu-relations

IceBreakers 2: Retreat Makers – Building Relationships

PURPOSE:
As teachers, we have been given the greatest gift…the power to change lives. Your classroom may be the only place where your students feel comfortable enough to learn life lessons and to build relationships. Give them the confidence by teaching students skills of how to act (and react) by making a connection between your program and the outside world.

REQUIREMENTS:
Slips of paper

PREPARATION:
Write situations or words on slips of paper for the students to role-play. Here are some suggestions:

Demonstrate a perfect rehearsal.
How do you demonstrate respect throughout the school day?
Why is discipline so necessary? What difference does it make in a musician's life?
Is having talent or heart more important to an ensemble?
The singers, dancers, band members, or director - who is needed most?
How do we improve audience etiquette?
How do you prepare for a solo audition? What is your response after it is announced?

DIRECTIONS:
1. Explain that each group will draw a slip of paper with a word or a statement.
2. Each small group will perform two short skits or simulations about the words on the chosen slip of paper. First, the group will act out the incorrect way to respond. Ask the rest of the class how they would change the skit for an outcome with an appropriate response. Give them a time limit for each.
3. Allow them several minutes to discuss their plan of action quietly.
4. Let the acting begin!
5. Afterwards, ask for responses from the other groups. Would they concur with the right and wrong responses? Would they offer any alternative solutions?

VARIATIONS:
There may be other situations that may arise during the year for the group and its members that don't necessarily involve music. Rehearse these situations so manners are modeled.

✓ Showing appropriate table manners at a post-performance banquet.
✓ Riding on a six-hour bus trip with 55 other musicians, chaperones, and teachers.
✓ Receiving a poor rating at contest when you were prepared to receive a 1+ rating.
✓ An important event is cancelled due to bad weather.
✓ Not getting the solo or part that you thought you should have received.
✓ Not "loving" some of the literature in your music folder.
✓ Noticing that the person next to you on stage has ripped his pants.
✓ Group leaders are expelled from school because of inappropriate choices.

ICE TIP:
Increase student engagement with interaction. The students may come up with ways to respond that are far better solutions than you ever imagined. Students will have ownership in this process and the next time a situation arises, you have equipped them with knowledge and experience. This is great P.R. for your department and your student will have gained invaluable life skills.

PURPOSE:

Warm Fuzzies will provide opportunities to students so they feel positive about themselves. It would be impossible to stop the encouraging and uplifting energy that will flow through your classroom room once this activity is completed. Maintain an attitude of acceptance and approval by celebrating and acknowledging each other's accomplishments. Remember, life isn't always about surviving storms but sometimes learning to dance in the rain.

REQUIREMENTS:

None

PREPARATION:

None

DIRECTIONS:

1. Ask students to sit in a circle.
2. Explain to the students that a warm fuzzy in the activity is recounting a time when they experienced something good, someone changed their life for good, or they caused something great to happen for someone else. How can they "pay it forward?"
3. Give a time limit.
4. Start the game by opening yourself up to the students with your own warm fuzzy experience. The instructor will set the tone of the game. If done correctly, this activity can do amazing things to energize the rest of the rehearsal or class period.
5. Moving around the circle, ask the students to share a recent time when they experienced a warm fuzzy feeling. If they have problems coming up with something, ask them to share a warm fuzzy about someone else in the circle without mentioning names.
6. After each turn, the rest of the class rubs their hands together (creating a warm feeling) and then responds with "snaps," alternately snapping fingers.

VARIATIONS:

- **Warm Glowing Fuzzies** Using candles, pass around the light as each person reveals his "feeling good" info. Start this activity in the dark, with only one lit candle. As each person encourages and shares positive accolades, he will pass the flame until the entire room is glowing. In the words of singer, James Taylor, "Shed a Little Light." It can change a person's outlook on life!
- **One Warm Word** Are you in a real time crunch? Allow the students a one-word warm fuzzy.
- **Fuzzy Bear Fuzzies** Give each student a gummy bear. The students respond according to the candy's color.

ICE TIP:

This game was created in one of the last showchoir rehearsals of the year. The students were sad about the year ending and saying goodbyes. This icebreaker truly added positive energy to the rehearsal and the ensemble strengthened their already deep bonds and connections with one another. It is now a tradition with our showchoir.

Thank you, Lanie Ellis and the 2008 Butler Headliners, for creating and sharing your warm glowing fuzzies with all of us!

venn connections

IceBreakers 2: Retreat Makers – Building Relationships

PURPOSE:
Three people will connect while student engagement increases through interaction. In addition, **Venn Connections** will give each student a chance to sing his own praises and put it into writing!

REQUIREMENTS:
Paper (as many sheets needed for the different versions)

PREPARATION:
Prepare the Venn diagrams on sheets of paper with three circles that intersect.

DIRECTIONS:
1. Tell the class that the goal of this icebreaker is to form a new trio (three students) every three minutes and find something that all three have in common.
2. Insist that class members find a common connection (music is not an acceptable answer in this game.) The students elected to be involved in this class, so encourage them to think outside the box – literally! All responses must be POSITIVE! Challenge them to find connectors that might be out of the ordinary like an unusual hobby, beloved sports team, favorite dessert, fast food menu item, hangout spot in the local mall, favorite boy band, favorite type of weather, or number of broken bones.
    a. Something all three have in common.
    b. Something two of the crew have in common.
    c. A special talent that only one possesses.
3. The three students must write the commonalities on the Venn diagram.
4. In the event the trio can not think of something they have in common, give suggestions.

VARIATIONS:
- **Teacher + You** Pair up the students. A third person (teacher, accompanist, choreographer) will not actually interact with the duo, but the duo will speculate the adult's answers. The students write the answers down and then establish which group comes up with the right answers. Consider what the students have in common with the chosen adult and what talents the adult possesses that the students may not. Discuss how each would fit in a newly formed trio.
- **The Circle of Life** Use this icebreaker as a take-home assignment for students to complete with family members.

ICE TIPS:
- Post the Venn diagrams publicly so students can see how their likes and dislikes compare with others.
- Try this icebreaker at a faculty meeting or with staff who deal with your students on a daily basis (for example, the custodian, cafeteria staff, librarian, secretary, PTA President).

nature calls

IceBreakers 2: Retreat Makers – Building Relationships

PURPOSE:
Nature Calls, an indoor or outside icebreaker, gives students practice helping each other and asking for others' help to resolve differences. If you want to succeed, you must operate as a team.

REQUIREMENTS:
A large area of space
Four pieces of paper with one of the four seasons written on each sheet
Nature items include:
- WINTER = snowballs (20 styrofoam balls)
- SPRING = flowers (20 pieces of brightly colored paper)
- SUMMER = sunshine (20 yellow balloons)
- AUTUMN = leaves (20 pieces of wadded up colored tissue paper used for packages)

PREPARATION:
Tape off a large area of space into four equal sections, labeling each section as one of the seasons (Winter, Spring, Summer, Autumn). Divide the nature items evenly into the center of the four quadrants so there will be five styrofoam balls, five pieces of colored paper, five balloons, and five pieces of colored tissue wrapping in each section.

DIRECTIONS:
1. Divide class into four equal teams, give each group a sheet of paper with one of the seasons written at the top, and instruct each group to find their season and sit in a circle around the nature props in their section.
2. Hand each group their particular piece of paper listing their season.
3. Inform students when music begins, each group tries to get the other seasons' nature items out of their quadrant, while keeping their nature item and collecting their nature items from the other sections in the following ways:
   a. WINTER = *Throw* snowballs (using hands to get the styrofoam out of the area)
   b. SPRING = *Grow* flowers (using feet to kick colored paper out of the area)
   c. SUMMER = *Glow* sunshine (using heads to bump balloons out of the area)
   d. AUTUMN = *Blow* leaves (using air to blow the wadded tissues out of the area)
4. When one "seasoned" team gets all of the other seasons' elements of nature *out* of their area and the correct nature items *in* their quadrant, that team is declared winners.

VARIATION:
If time is an issue, use four colors of balloons to represent the four seasons. Each time the music stops, give new directions on how to move the "items from nature." Ideas could include kicking, blowing, head and hip bumping.

ICE TIP:
Use background music. Here are some suggestions:
- Classical music lovers should try Vivaldi's "The Four Seasons"
- '60s fans should sample Frankie Valli and The Four Seasons
- Light humor will be provided with the recording of P.D.Q. Bach's "Seasonings"
- Broadway fans will enjoy "Seasons of Love" (from the musical, "Rent").

heads up! singer's up!

IceBreakers 2: Retreat Makers – Building Relationships

PURPOSE:
Do you remember the game, "Head's Up, Seven Up?" Used in classrooms today, some of the "experienced" teachers have probably played this game in their youth. **Heads Up! Singer's Up!** is a remixed version for the musically-inclined scholars. Students sing individually while experimenting with the sounds, timbres, and ranges of their voice.

REQUIREMENTS:
Desks or tables for students to put their heads down

PREPARATION:
Predetermined list of familiar songs (i.e. "Happy Birthday," children's nursery rhymes, an approved radio song, or perhaps a piece of repertoire you are working on in chorus).

DIRECTIONS:
1. Students can either sit in desks, or tables in a big circle.
2. Each round, seven students will be chosen as the first singing group. They will be given the job of tapping someone's thumb and singing a predetermined song into that person's ear. Encourage the students to disguise their voices by changing the timbre, tone, and presentation to confuse the listener.
3. Instruct the students who are seated to close their eyes, form a fist with the thumb pointed in the air.
4. After all students have eyes closed, heads lowered, and thumbs into position, the "chosen seven" tap seven other students lightly on the shoulder to go around the room and sing in someone's ear.
5. After each of the seven has performed, he or she will tiptoe to the front of the room.
6. Give the verbal cue, "Heads up!" and the remaining class can sit up and open eyes.
7. Those students who had their thumb pressed and a serenade sung in their ear will all stand and guess which classmate sung in their ears.
8. If they guess correctly, they replace the person in the next round's singing group. If they guess incorrectly, they must sit down and the singer gets another chance.

VARIATION:
Holiday Heads Up! Here's a great activity to play at any holiday party. Choose a song that corresponds with a specific holiday. Prepare a list of holiday and seasonal tunes.

ICE TIP:
This activity is quick and to the point. This icebreaker can be adapted to any situation and is a great warm-up activity at a retreat where students bond much quicker with the instructor and their classmates because they are involved. Not only are kids singing independently while experimenting with the sound of their own voice, this shifts the focus of singing "solo" to a fun guessing game of solving the mystery of "whose voice was that anyway?" *Thanks, Zane!*

PURPOSE:
This is the time to recognize individuals for the positive and good they contribute to your ensemble. Musical directors tend to focus over 95% of a rehearsal on the imperfect (wrong notes, incorrect embouchures, poor dynamics, faulty phrasing, un-stylistic, little musicality, etc). Use **Bravissimo!** to focus on the positive. It will have a huge impact on the individual and on his future attitude and success in your program.

REQUIREMENTS:
There are unlimited ways, big or small, to show appreciation, but it will take some effort on your part. Many times a sticky note with the word, *Bravissimo!* can change someone's day.

PREPARATION:
Decide ahead of time what kind of items to have ready.
A checklist of students' names

DIRECTIONS:
1. Pull this icebreaker out several times a year (retreat, around a campfire, seated in the classroom, a "pep talk" before a performance, end of the year) to address each of your students gifts and efforts.
   a. Talk to each student individually or address the entire class.
   b. Encourage classmates to show their appreciation of one another. Set guidelines so Bravo notes are done correctly and more importantly, that no one is left out.
   c. If your students are not comfortable giving out notes, keep *Bravissimo!* sticky notes handy and write a note on each one about each person. Pair up the notes with a name brand item. For example, add a roll of Smarties® candies to let the student know you think she is smart or attach a cinnamon Jolly Rancher® to tell the student how "fired-up" you are to have him in your program.
   d. Assign each student a "music bud," a classmate to observe during the rehearsal or retreat. The music buds can write positive notes to each other.
2. Always keep some treats or bravo notes handy for times when they could really make a difference for one of your students.

VARIATIONS:
The sky is the limit on this icebreaker. It is amazing how loyal students will be for a teacher they love and respect. It is like a mirror when that respect and love are returned.

ICE TIPS:
- Be specific about the accomplishment. Almost 30 years ago, my dance teacher, Miss Mary, gave me a written note after a dance rehearsal. I still have that note. I don't think she realized what that one simple note did for me. It's never too late to say thank you (Thanks, Miss Mary).
- Make sure that every student in your music program is acknowledged sometime during the year.

simple bravissimo! and "break-a-leg" ideas

IceBreakers 2: Retreat Makers – Building Relationships

Gathering these items may take some planning ahead, but students will be thrilled with your kind thoughts and actions. Many of your students will save the notes and little goodies for years. Corrections can help, but encouragement can even be a far greater help.

DIRECTIONS:

Type a note and place in a cellophane gift bag or a baggy (individually wrapped and still affordable for the director). Choose one or several of the following ideas. Parent groups could also help in collecting and distributing the "break-a-leg" notes and goodies.
- Atomic Fireball® - to light your fire when you feel burned out
- Band-Aid® - to remember to be kind and to not hurt each other
- Cinnamon candy – to stay "fired up" for the program
- Emery board – remember that when the going gets rough, you have friends you can turn to
- Eraser - to remind you that everyone makes mistakes, but friends (and music teachers) forgive
- Gum – for "chews"-ing to be in this musical ensemble and to remind you to stick with it
- Hershey® Hug and Kiss and Gummy Bears®- to remind you that you are loved.
- Laffy Taffy® - to remind you to take time to laugh
- Million Dollar® candy bar with a note "This is what you are really worth!"
- Musketeers® - to remind you that teamwork can be sweet!
- Payday® candy bar for accompanist, band members, and volunteers. "...Wish it could be more!"
- Penny - to always use good "cents"
- Peppermint – to remind you of your daily commit-"mint"
- Q-Tip® - to remind you to be a good listener
- Smarties® - Fine Arts students are the smartest around!
- Starburst® – to remind you to reach for the STARS
- Sunflower seeds or Planters® peanuts – to remind you to grow where you have been planted
- Teabag – because you are "tea"-rrific!
- Tea candle or birthday candle – to keep lighting the way for future students
- Tootsie Roll® – remember to be a "roll/role" model at all times
- Whoppers® - to remind you to always tell the truth

FAVORITE QUOTES TO SHARE WITH STUDENTS AND STAFF:
1. The woods would be silent if no birds sang, except the best!
2. Giving it another try is better than an alibi.
3. The smallest good deed is better than the grandest intention.
4. Looking at the bright side of things never hurt anyone's eyes.
5. Perfect practice makes perfect performance.
6. If you find a path without obstacles, chances are it doesn't lead anywhere!
7. To be happy, think happy!
8. Anytime's the right time for learning something new.
9. Success is a balance of hard work and talents.
10. Be a "fun-to-be-with" person but always make wise choices.
11. Believe in yourself. If you don't, no one else will either.
12. Practice and determination make a winning combination.
13. Problems are challenges in disguise.
14. A little extra effort turns "good" into "best!"
15. A smile is a gift you can give every day. ☺

BONUS QUOTES:

"We are what we repeatedly do; Excellence, then, is not an act, but a habit." ~ Aristotle

"To sing well and dance well is to be well-educated." ~ Plato

what's your ring tone?

PURPOSE:
This is a great way to know students even better and a way to welcome technology into the classroom. In most classes (and syllabi), cell phones, I-pods, and MP3 players are not allowed. Set aside one day for students to bring in any and all of the above. Prove to students that you, the instructor, don't fear but rather embrace technology. However, there is a time and place for everything. Explain the school's policy on cell phone usage in class and how, when used improperly, the technology can disrupt the learning process.

REQUIREMENTS:
Students' cell phones (only the students with free unlimited talk time)

PREPARATION:
None

DIRECTIONS:
1. Choose 5-10 students to bring their cell phones to the front of the room.
2. Ask other students in the class to call the phones that are up front. See if the students can coordinate their efforts to get the cell phones to ring simultaneously.
3. Can class members decipher the ring tones? Ask students to guess which ring tone belongs to which fellow classmate.
4. If hearing all the rings at once is too difficult of a task for the class, call the phones one at a time to clearly hear the ring tone.
5. When a student guesses correctly, the ring tone owner explains why they chose that ring tone.

For example, my ring tone is Barry Manilow's "Copacabana." I chose this ring tone because:
   a) Very few people have the ring tone so I don't confuse my ring with others'.
   b) It is a catchy melody, upbeat and it makes me smile.
   c) I am a Barry Fan-i-low, much to the students' chagrin.

VARIATIONS:
• Use this day to discuss classroom cell phone etiquette and audience etiquette. How do you feel when you are on stage and everyone in the audience is texting or talking on their phones? As performers, how can we prevent this and train our audiences to show better etiquette?
• How can we solve the problem? In my classes, if a cell phone goes off (accidentally or not), the entire 90-voice Concert Choir yells, "Treats!" Believe me, after bringing homemade treats for 90 choir members, that student never again forgets to turn off their cell phone before coming to Concert Choir.

ICE TIP:
Determine how to get all the phones to ring at the same time. Ask a student to talk about something in which they are passionate about. See how they feel when they are competing with the cell phone noise. Come up with a solution, as a class, so everyone has some ownership in the final decision. Encourage them to share cell phone etiquette information with families and friends.

meaningful initials

IceBreakers 2: Life Lessons – Establishing Respect

PURPOSE:
Students will not only learn classmates' names, but they'll discover some interesting facts about each person. English teachers will thank you for the use of acronyms and the creative writing assignment.

REQUIREMENTS:
One piece of paper per student
Writing utensils

PREPARATION:
None

DIRECTIONS:
1. Hand out a sheet of paper and one writing utensil per student.
2. Ask them to write their name vertically down the left side of the paper in capital letters.
3. Encourage them to think creatively for an adjective or an activity that starts with each letter of their names that accurately describes them (if a student's name is less than five letters, encourage him to use his last name). All adjectives completing the acronym must be positive and complimentary in nature!
4. Each student should write the adjectives down.
5. Next, each student stands to offer a short explanation why she chose the adjectives or activities to describe herself.

Example:
   A = Airplanes are my favorite way to travel.
   L = Lindsay is Alex's girlfriend.
   E = Eagle Scout (Alex is an Eagle Scout).
   X = EXcited (same sound) about choir this year!

VARIATIONS:
- **Initial Those Initials** If time is short, use the student's initials.
- **First and Last Initials** Do you have extra time? Use both first and last names.
- **Middle Initials** Use in the middle of the year as an exercise to learn middle names.
- **Musical Initials** Each student must come up with musical terms (notes, rests, dynamics, tempo, composers, etc.) for each letter of his name. Make this assignment broad enough that the student can be creative (i.e. favorite singer, musical style, band, instrument, choice musical selection, or Broadway show). Challenge your students to think musically and allow them to share some of their musical knowledge with the instructor and the class. You may be surprised what and how much you will learn!
- **Instructor Initials** Teach students to spell the teacher's name correctly.

ICE TIPS:
- If using this icebreaker with younger children, give a few examples for each alphabet letter.
- Display the meaningful acronyms for parents and for students to see.

don't squash my butterfly!

IceBreakers 2: Life Lessons – Establishing Respect

PURPOSE:
Teach to build a positive environment. Nothing can endanger the spirit of a choir more than negativism. This icebreaker will make students aware of how negative words can shut down communication while teaching students to discuss in a positive manner. True leaders learn how to listen and to build up those around them, not to tear down.

REQUIREMENTS:
None

PREPARATION:
None

DIRECTIONS:
1. Pair up students, designating an "A" and a "B" student.
2. Post three dialogue topics. The pair chooses one to discuss.
   a. A concert they wish to attend.
   b. The newest techno-gadget each wants to purchase.
   c. What are weekend plans?
3. Inform the students that the "A" student will try to dialogue with his partner. The "B" partner will intentionally interrupt with negative comments ("Yes, but…," "I don't think I can because…," or perhaps "I would if only…."
4. Allow two minutes for the interaction and then allow another two minutes for the pair to switch tasks.
5. At the end of the second round, tell the pairs to return to the same conversations, using only positive language (no "buts," "ifs," or "I don't think I can" statements in any of the sentences).
6. Open a class discussion about the reaction to both the positive and negative directives and then each pair can share their dialogue with the rest of the class.

VARIATIONS:
Lead a discussion on a group trip, an upcoming tour, a rehearsal, or a performance and let each person say something with the "yes, but…," "I would if…," and "I don't think I can" lingo. This quickly destroys the positive class atmosphere. Try the same conversation around the circle using only positive dialogue. Can you and your students hear to the difference? After finishing both discussions, point out improved body language, facial responses, enhanced energy levels, vocal pitches, and the speed of the delivery. How much difference did it make to put a positive spin on these exchanges of dialogue?

ICE TIPS:
- Secretly videotape this exercise to show students so they can re-experience their conversations. Ask if they remember their negative response. Ask them to consider how they think teachers, parents, and friends view their answers.
- Dialogue is a two-way street. Continually telling someone else what to do can ruin any relationship.

energizing envelopes

IceBreakers 2: Life Lessons – Establishing Respect

PURPOSE:
Getting positive feedback from friends and teachers is one of the best motivators for a student.

REQUIREMENTS:
One large envelope for each student
Many strips of paper
Writing utensils

PREPARATION:
None

DIRECTIONS:
1. Ask students to sit in a circle and pass each a large envelope and a writing utensil.
2. Instruct students to write their first name (and last initial if multiple students with the same name) clearly on the front of the envelope.
3. Explain that in each 30 second round, each student will accept the passed envelope, write something positive about the student on one of the strips of paper, put it back in the envelope and pass the envelope to his right on the cue.
4. To insure there are only positive statements or encouragements, inform students that the envelopes will be picked up at the end of the icebreaker and all of the contents will be read before they are returned to the owners.
5. Again, do not let students read the contents of the envelope at that time. They will eagerly anticipate getting the envelope and you have an incentive for good behavior.

VARIATION:
Wait for the right moment to share the **Energizing Envelopes**. Mail out the envelopes when you feel a student needs a little pick-me-up. Give the envelope as a holiday gift, at the end of a retreat, or as a graduation gift. This strategy will be a great help with retention for the upcoming year. Positive feedback is always appreciated and helps the morale of the class.

ICE TIPS:
- Try this activity as a thank you for a staff member who is not usually recognized (a custodian, a cafeteria worker, an accompanist, a student teacher, a secretary, or anyone who has earned and would benefit from recognition. Positive words can be life changing and can give school personnel the added encouragement to "keep on, keepin' on."
- Keep an "under-the-desk box" with positive notes from students. Rough day? After reading the notes aloud, the mood and the atmosphere will improve.

talent chain!

PURPOSE:
Discover and share the students' "rainbow" of talents. This experience allows students to physically acknowledge and write about special talents they possess. They'll be reminded that the group can be stronger than the individual and that there are no weak links in this chain of talent!

REQUIREMENTS:
Colored paper strips • Writing utensils

PREPARATION:
None

DIRECTIONS:
1. Pass out a writing utensil and 3-5 colored strips of paper to each student.
2. On each strip of paper, tell the student to write his initials on one side of the paper and a special talent he possesses on the other side (one talent per each strip of paper).
3. If there is a lull of ideas, remind each of some of the great gifts each possesses or the many contributions each makes to the ensemble or the class (see the list below).
4. Collect all strips, match the ends to create a circle, and link them to create a chain.
5. Decorate the classroom with the talent chain and encourage students to look at the rainbow of talent often.

VARIATION:
Hopeless Chain Ask students to write one thing they don't like about themselves. Collect each strip and either shred it or burn it (if allowed in a retreat situation) in front of the student. Inspire each person to let go of the negativity and focus on where they can grow and what they can fix. Life is too short to focus on the bad. Wipe the slate clean and look forward to the future.

ICE TIPS:
• Alarmingly, students can quickly come up with all of their faults and point out what is wrong with themselves and others. This activity provides the opportunity to help individuals see what makes him special and focus on strengths.
• If you work hard as a team, you can achieve anything. Lessons learned?
    a) The group is stronger than the individual.
    b) The class is full of talented individuals – a virtual rainbow of talent.
    c) A person can accomplish anything if they work hard enough.
    d) There is a support system already in place.

Remind students (and faculty members) of the talents they possess:
Musical, academic, or athletic talents, organization, dedication, determination, great attitude, great aptitude, energy, smile on face, good friend, supportive, positive, optimistic, encourager, happy person, sees best in others, imaginative, resourceful, productive, helpful, rule follower, fun, sense of humor, high morals, good person, creative, great dancer, good rapper, computer wiz, friendly, on time, math wiz, great memory, not afraid to try, great facial expressions, social, animated, poised, self-confident, kind spirit, caring, compassionate, thoughtful, gentle, not bossy, never tattles, stands up for what is right, big-hearted, doesn't give up, doesn't complain, great leader, great follower, passionate, excels in school, shining star, independent, artistic, works well with others, etc.

nicknames

IceBreakers 2: Life Lessons – Establishing Respect

PURPOSE:
This non-threatening activity allows students to revisit their childhood and share a nickname given to them by family members or friends. *In all icebreaker activities, students have the option to share or to not participate at that time.

REQUIREMENTS:
None

PREPARATION:
Be prepared to share your own childhood nickname and the story behind the name.

DIRECTIONS:
1. Ask class members to share a childhood nickname that was given to them from a family member, a friend, a peer, or a small child who could not pronounce their given name.
2. Start out by sharing your own childhood nickname and its story.
3. Ask for volunteers to share their own nicknames and the back stories behind each.
4. In conclusion, discuss nicknames. How and why was the name given? Was it deserved? Is there anyone else with the same nickname? Can nicknames be harmful? Can nicknames ever be positive? Why do we often outgrow the nicknames?
5. What is a nickname you desired as a child?
6. How does the media use nicknames?

VARIATIONS:
- If there are two students with the same name in class, how do they want to be individually identified? The class might have a Kate, a Katie, and the Kate-ster.
- Be prepared with a written (or mental) list of positive character traits for every student in your classroom. If a student isn't able to recall a childhood nickname, make up one for him on the spot. Be careful not to let the class participate in this as their idea of a complimentary name might not be the same as yours. How does each student want to be addressed in class?

ICE TIP:
Ask students to list a nickname they would like on the back of a T-shirt or jacket. Save this list. As an end-of-the-year project, students can decorate T-shirts for each other using the "wished for" nickname. If T-shirts are cost-prohibitive, plastic cups, small plastic frames, and markers can be purchased inexpensively. Present the nickname gifts on the last day of class. Demonstrate your well wishes by remembering something about your students and they will make a point to remember you and will more than likely tell their friends and siblings to enroll and audition for your program.

I C E B R E A K E R S

PURPOSE:
Variety is the spice of life. What a boring lot we would be if we all thought and acted just alike. Aren't you glad that everyone in the class is not just like you? What would rehearsals be like if everyone was like you and there were not any differing opinions? Use this exercise to work out differences and maintain an attitude of acceptance.

REQUIREMENTS:
None

PREPARATION:
None

DIRECTIONS:
1. Split the class into smaller groups (around five people each). Purposefully separate like-minded individuals.
2. Give the groups a few minutes for introductions and to share some information about themselves.
3. Explain that each small group will be hypothetically going to Iceland for the winter. In the allotted time, they discuss and agree upon ten items that will fit into a suitcase.
4. Ask them to prioritize the ten items. Group members must be able to defend the items' ranking to the other groups.
5. Bring the class back together to discuss how easy or difficult the assignment. Did a leader emerge? Who became the group's secretary? Were there any members who chose not to participate? How were disagreements between students handled?

VARIATION:
B.T.Y.N. This is an acronym for one of my favorite sayings, "Breath through your nose." It is physically impossible to breathe through your nose and talk at the same time. Partners take turns telling a partner about a favorite piece of music or a group while the listener of the pair practices B.T.Y.N. Switch places. Isn't it nice to dialogue without interruptions?

ICE TIP:
What is the difference between discussion and dialogue? Discussion is from the same Latin root that the words *percussion* and *concussion* come from, whereas the word dialogue comes from the Latin word *logos*, meaning "God-inspired." When we dialogue, we listen to the person speaking without preconceived ideas. The language of leadership is dialogue – exchanging ideas, not forcing one's opinions on another person. What unites a team or an ensemble more than anything else is a common purpose. Let people know upfront what you stand for and what you won't stand for!

more headliner questions

IceBreakers 2: Life Lessons – Establishing Respect

PURPOSE:
My first book, ***Icebreakers: 60 Fun Activities That Will Build a Better Choir***, contained a section called "Headliner Questions." Dr. Eph Ehly, author of ***Hogey's Journey*** and sought after choral conductor, noted that he enjoyed reading these questions with his grandchildren. Other educators have used the Headliner questions at rehearsal dinners (bride and groom families getting to know each other), family reunions, youth group functions, teacher in-services, church choir rehearsals, long car rides, and a host of other events. Here are a few more questions that you can add to the list. Enjoy...

REQUIREMENTS:
A list of Headliner questions

PREPARATION:
None

DIRECTIONS:
Play as listed in the original ***Icebreakers***. Here are 20 additional questions (from silly to serious):
1. What is your favorite knock-knock joke? Tell it, punch line and all.
2. If you were talking in your sleep, what would you say?
3. Where is the worst place you have been stuck waiting? How long did you wait?
4. Favorite flavor of jellybean? Favorite combination of jellybeans?
5. If every time you entered a room, a theme song played, what would that song be?
6. If you were a super hero, what would your power be?
7. What Disney® character would you like to eliminate?
8. What was the weirdest thing you have ever eaten? Would you eat it again?
9. What ice cream flavor would you invent?
10. What is your favorite pie, vegetable, type of art work, recess activity, rock band?
11. What are three things that could improve this department; this school; or you personally?
12. If you could cheat on a test and not be caught, would you? Would you let a friend cheat?
13. If you could go to another country, but knew you would never return, would you go? Undersea? Outer space?
14. Your friend made you a personalized t-shirt, but you don't care for it. Do you wear it?
15. If you get too much change back, do you tell the cashier or a manager? Or would you keep the change? If you found a wallet with $500 what would you do?
16. Would you rather be a famous actor or solve the nation's financial problems?
17. If you were only given six months to live, what would you do first?
18. If elected President of the U.S.A, what would you change? What would scare you the most about the presidency? Who would be your Vice President?
19. Who was your best teacher and why?
20. What would you like to ask God?

ICE TIPS: Here is a list of interviewer Barbara Walter's five favorite questions:
• If recuperating in a hospital, with whom would you want to share your hospital room?
• What was your first job? How much were you paid?
• When was the last time you cried? Laughed 'til you cried?
• Who was the first person (or thing) you ever loved?
• What has made you the happiest this past year?

PURPOSE:
Students construct silver trophies for fellow classmates acknowledging the strengths and talents of their peers. This is a great way to give recognition and to celebrate everyone's effort.

REQUIREMENTS:
Aluminum foil
Slips of paper
Balloons (optional)

PREPARATION:
Write the name of a student on a slip of paper. Be sure to include everyone. Precut the aluminum foil.

DIRECTIONS:
1. Hand out one slip with a student's name to each student.
2. Give each participant a large piece of aluminum foil (20" x 20"). More foil is available upon request.
3. Give the students five minutes to create a silver trophy for the person whose name was on the slip of paper.
4. At the end of class, conduct an awards ceremony when the students will present the "winning prizes" to the recipients and will offer explanation behind the award.

VARIATIONS:
- **And The Trophy Goes To...** Let each section or small group create a trophy for another section. Display the prizes in the room as motivating decorations. The woodwind section could create a trophy for the percussionists and the brass for the string section. The altos create a trophy for the tenors, and so forth. Give regulations before the trophies are created. Ask the artists to add a plaque with the "award-winning" group's name.
- **Balloon Trophy** Twist and tie several long balloons (the type that clowns use to make balloon animals) together to represent a trophy of some sort.
- **Traveling Trophy** Challenge students to create a trophy to display on a shelf in the classroom. Award it each year to a deserving student. Allow students to vote the most improved or hardest working classmate.

ICE TIP:
Ask the winners to give an acceptance speech the next day. Who will they thank? Challenge classmates to use encouraging words without a trophy on an everyday basis. It is fun to be recognized. Be sure everyone is included.

new year's "party time"

IceBreakers 2: Holiday Games – Celebrating Special Occasions

PURPOSE:
Creating a time capsule gives students motivation to set goals, revisit the past, and look ahead into the future.

REQUIREMENTS:
Shoe boxes or empty tissue boxes
Aluminum foil
Paper
Writing utensils

PREPARATION:
Ask students to bring empty shoe boxes or tissue boxes on a designated day or collect boxes throughout the year.

DIRECTIONS:
1. Issue students an empty shoe box or tissue box, aluminum foil, markers, and paper.
2. Students will construct a time capsule from the materials provided. The student must write down five resolutions. After each resolution, the student must write one way to achieve that specific goal.
3. Collect the time capsules.
4. Wait for the perfect time to share the time capsule with the student.

EXAMPLES:
Goal: I want to reduce stress in my life.
Plan: Find time to take a yoga class, turn off the TV, or have daily quiet time.

Goal: I want to learn to play the guitar.
Plan: Find a good guitar teacher, rent a guitar, and commit to practice.

Goal: I want to save money for college
Plan: Make a budget, visit the school counselor, and strive for scholarship-winning grades.

VARIATION:
Class Time Capsule As a final gift, give the capsules to your students as a graduating gift or ask them to visit after graduation (plus this will eliminate mailing costs), giving them another reason to visit the music class! If a student is moving or is enrolling in a different school, give them the gift as a parting gift.

ICE TIPS:
Use the phrases in the time capsule:
- Our future belongs to those who believe in the beauty of dreaming.
- Shoot for the moon, and even if you miss it, you will land among the stars.
- Our imagination is the only limit to what we can hope to have in the future.
- Yesterday's the past and tomorrow's the future. Today is a gift, which is why it is called the present.
- I'm having the time of my life.
- There is a right time for everything...(Ecclesiastes 3: 1-8)
- "The best thing about the future is that it only comes one day at a time." – *Abraham Lincoln*

PURPOSE:
The month of February can be difficult as some students may feel left out on Valentine's Day. Instead of focusing on the romance, use this icebreaker to value friendship and remember the kindness that surrounds them. Use the holiday to teach respect, how to appreciate their peers, and how powerful words and actions can be to someone.

REQUIREMENTS:
One piece of white paper for each student
One piece of red paper for each student
Scissors (several students can share)
Scotch tape (several students can share)

PREPARATION:
None

DIRECTIONS:
1. Distribute two different colored sheets of paper to each person.
2. Instruct students to cut a large paper doll out of the white paper.
3. Next, ask students to cut out a large heart out of the red paper.
4. Shred the paper doll into as many pieces as desired (don't tell students the next step until they are done shredding their paper dolls).
5. Challenge class members to use the scotch tape to piece the doll back together.
6. Discuss the lesson that ugly words or actions can be sharper than a knife. Once something is said, it can not be taken back.
7. Using the red heart, invite the students to write one word or a short sentence about what they think is important in a friendship.

VARIATION:
Hearts For Special People Ask the class to decide on a recipient (school personnel, staff, accompanist, parent volunteers, etc.) for this icebreaker. Use a large piece of paper to draw a large heart. Decorate the heart with colored pencils or sharpies. Each student writes a positive word or a short sentence about why that person is special. All members of the class should sign the heart. Deliver with a little sack of Valentine candy or a carnation flower. Giving thanks during the holidays is a great way to build relationships and say thank you on this special day. Write a Valentine ditty so it becomes a singing Valentine-gram.

ICE TIP:
Friends can try to put us back together after a bad word or experience, but we are never quite the same. Be careful of what you say to friends. Keep the red paper heart as a reminder of what it takes to be a good friend.

land o' green

IceBreakers 2: Holiday Games – Celebrating Special Occasions

PURPOSE:
"Think green!" This game can be used for St. Patrick's' Day, Earth Day, or for both holidays. Some of your students will catch on quickly and some will want more time to figure out the game and solution.

REQUIREMENTS:
None

PREPARATION:
None

DIRECTIONS:
1. Share a riddle with your class to decipher.
   Invite your students to the land of green. Individuals will ask questions and try to get "into the land of green." Only if they decipher the riddle (having to do with double consonants) can they enter. You will then say, "Yes, Kristina. You can enter the land of green," or "Sorry, try again."

In the land of green there are kittens but no cats, spoons but no forks, moons but no suns, and grass but no shrubbery. Can you join me in the land of green?

2. If you can not figure out the riddle, ask one of your students to share the answer. Seriously, many times the obvious is right in front of us. Asking a student for help with the riddle also gives the student a sense of pride and ownership. If the answer is in print, "enemy hands" could uncover it and share the solution which then ruins the element of surprise. Give additional hints to younger students.

VARIATIONS:
- **This is the Game of Snaps** This is a great travel game. This game was recently featured in the credits of the movie, "P.S. I Love You." Watch the credits for the answer.
- **Assassins** Off the license tag in front of us, off the steering wheel, off the tissue box, who is it?
- **My Aunt Emma Died, Did She Die?** Now listen, again for the answer...
- **Black Magic!** Is it the silver stand? No. Is it the black folder? No. Is it the green plant? Yes!
- **My Cow (Counting Cows)**. But if you see a graveyard, you lose all your cow points. A church and your points are doubled. Great activity for long bustrips.
- **Zip or No Zip** This is a counting and observation game. As a native Kansan, I can spot windmills quite easily. This game may not work in your part of the country, so substitute "golden arches" or whatever is accessible in your neck of the woods.

ICE TIP:
Find these brainteasers and other fun riddles online or in riddle books. My students love them because they're fun and I love them because I see the students having real interaction instead of closing out the world with the earphones. Have a series of games ready for your next party!

For more information on riddles and tour games, check online or
contact the publisher for my information.
www.shawneepress.com

PURPOSE:
Similar to an Easter egg hunt, this icebreaker can only happen in cold weather climates because colored ice cubes are used.

REQUIREMENTS:
Cold weather, snow, or ice
Colored ice cubes
Baggies

PREPARATION:
Prepare colored ice cubes made with food coloring or Kool-Aid®. Use various colors that are appropriate for the celebrated holiday (red for Valentine's Day, green for St. Patrick's Day or multi-colored ice cubes for Easter).

Allow time to hide ice cubes in the snow or ice.

DIRECTIONS:
1. Challenge students to find hidden colored ice cubes as individuals or as teams.
2. As the ice cubes are discovered, the students place them in plastic baggies.
3. Once a student has found their designated allotment of colored ice cubes, she presents her baggie of colored ice cubes for a prize.
4. Discard all baggies with colored, melted ice cubes in a large trashcan.

VARIATIONS:
Eggs-Words Write a note and place it inside a plastic egg replacing the prefix "ex" with "eggs."

Eggs-words: extra, extract, extracurricular, extraneous, extraordinary, extravagant, extreme, exuberant, exude, exultant, expulsion, explosive, express, example, exploit, explain, extend, exercise, extra, exact, exaggerate, exclaim, exclude, excuse, exemplary, expert, explode, exalt, exam, exasperate, exceed, excel, excellence, except, exchange, excess, excite, excitement, exhausted, exhibit, exist, expense, etc.

An example of a note placed in plastic Easter eggs and hidden in choir folders.

Words cannot eggs-press what an eggs-traordinary time we've had this choir season. We want to eggs-tend our gratitude to each and every one of you for eggs-pending your eggs-cellent gifts and eggs-hibiting love through this eggs-citing and eggs-ellent message. We pray that this eggs-perience was not too eggs-hausting, but rather an eggs-alting eggs-ercise in Faith. Thanks for being such an eggs-tra, eggs-uberant, and eggs-emplary member!

Have a Hoppy Eggs-ster! ~Your Egg-stra Special Choir Directors

ICE TIPS:
- Remind students to bring mittens and dress accordingly for the outside project. This game only works for people in cold climates. No matter what the weather, or age of student, Easter egg hunts are egg-citing and an egg-cellent way to celebrate the holiday!
- It's an inexpensive treat, but a priceless activity for appreciative members.

april falling fools

IceBreakers 2: Holiday Games – Celebrating Special Occasions

PURPOSE:
A great physical stretching icebreaker, this one will make your students "fall" for the gag.

REQUIREMENTS:
Space

PREPARATION:
None

DIRECTIONS:
1. Pair up students who are about the same height and body type.
2. The first person is encouraged to relax, lying on his back with arms out to the side and his legs perpendicular in the air, so his body appears to make an "L-shape."
3. Instruct the person on the ground to close his eyes during this two minute icebreaker.
4. Speak quietly and try to get the person to totally relax during the allotted time.
5. Cue the standing partner to slowly lower the legs one inch at a time.
6. The person lying on the ground will experience a strange feeling as if his legs will fall through the floor long before they actually touch the ground.

VARIATIONS:
- **April "Falling on Face" Fools Game** One partner lies on the ground, faces downward with closed eyes, arms and legs extended, and hands and arms cover his ears. The partner stands straddling feet on either side of the partner's hips. Both bodies are facing the same direction. The standing partner picks up the arms of the partner on the ground and stretches the body for 30-90 seconds. The standing partner slowly lowers the body to the floor. Another strange feeling of hitting the floor long before contact is made! *Do not let anyone try this version who has back problems as this proves to be a rigorous stretch.
- **Standing April Fools Game** Stand in an open door frame. Push hard on door for 90 seconds. Once the time is over, release. Astounding how arms seem to float up and you are unable to control the motion.
- **Shaking Hands April Fools** Clasp hands and index fingers, fingers intertwined. Lift index finger straight up as far as you can. Your body will begin to shake.

ICE TIPS:
- Sometimes April Fools pranks can be mean or past the point of silliness. These different stretching techniques, when done correctly, will "fool" your body.
- Ask students to share other April Fools pranks that are done without a prop (i.e. cracking an egg over your head, spiders running over the shoulders, or blowing a cold breath as if the wind is blowing).
- A person who stands for nothing will fall for anything and everything.
  (Told to me by Vaughn Lippoldt, the greatest prankster of all time)

PURPOSE:
Can I come to your party? This is a challenging game of observation skills.

REQUIREMENTS:
None

PREPARATION:
None

DIRECTIONS:
1. Ask participants to sit in a circle with or without chairs, and explain that you are going to have a party to which they may or may not be invited.
2. Encourage them to ask if they can come to the party and state what they will be wearing to the party.
3. The person who guesses on what basis you are allowing people to come then takes over the game. Answer according to criteria which you have previously established.

For example you may invite those:
- ✓ who say the word, "like" before asking if they can come to your party
- ✓ who ask to be invited when you have your feet crossed
- ✓ who have their feet crossed when they ask to be invited
- ✓ who are wearing a brand of shoes that ends with a vowel
- ✓ who ask to be invited by using your first and last name
- ✓ who will wear a certain color
- ✓ who laugh before asking if they come to the party

If they struggle, give a hint. For instance if you designated "wearing a brand of shoes that ends with a vowel," the response may be, "No Mandy, you cannot come wearing your Adidas® tennis shoes, but you can wear your Nike's®."

VARIATIONS:
- Ask students to form circles according to the month of their birthday (12 circles total). Don't tell students where to be seated. Each team can act out their birthday month.
- Answer the following questions.
  - ♪ What is the earliest memory of a birthday celebration?
  - ♪ What world events occurred the year of your birthday?
  - ♪ What is the best thing about being your age (and the hardest thing about being your age)?
  - ♪ What was your best year? What age are you most looking forward to?
  - ♪ Best birthday gift ever received?
  - ♪ What is your favorite birthday gift you've given to someone else?

ICE TIP:
Don't forget students with summer or holiday birthdays. Sing to all the students who celebrate during those times.

firecracker dance

IceBreakers 2: Holiday Games – Celebrating Special Occasions

PURPOSE:
Concentration, rhythm skills, listening, observing, and individually participating, are all covered in this activity that when done rapidly, sounds like fireworks.

REQUIREMENTS:
Space to make two to ten rows of people
Marching band music playing in the background (optional)

PREPARATION:
None

DIRECTIONS:
1. Divide students into straight lines, equal in length.
2. Tell the students that they will be passing a percussive sound from one student to the next from the front of the line to the back.
3. Allow the students a trial run. The game is easier than it seems!
4. Add on by asking students to "pass the snap" (snap their fingers) one person at a time.
5. Challenge them to move the sound down the line and then back to the front.
6. Add other percussive sounds (For example, add on a stomp. The snap will go down and back and then stomp down and back).
7. Add a clap to this pattern. The pattern gets longer and tougher to memorize.
8. Last, add a shout, "Yeah!"
9. The team who moves the body percussion down and back first is the winner. Make this more difficult by adding the rule that if they snap, clap, stomp, or yell out of turn, the whole line must start over.
10. For a fun experiment, try the exercise with eyes closed.

VARIATIONS:
- **States Dance** A great geographical icebreaker where students pretend the entire room is the United States of America. Instruct students to stand in the state or city where they were born. Next, they should move where their parents were born. This game teaches map skills and students will learn where fellow students hail.
- **Flag Day** Give each student a piece of paper with a state written on the front. Students should hold up the piece of paper in front of their chest when their turn comes (like the wave). Use this with patriotic songs or lyrics that mention various states in the U.S.A.
- **Yankee Doodle** Choose one student to be Yankee Doodle. This student will play detective and try to uncover which student (or state) is missing. Ask one person "Dandy" (or state) to leave the room. Can Yankee Doodle find his Dandy?

ICE TIPS:
- If the students can perfect and speed up the **Firecracker Dance**, this rhythmic pattern will sound like fireworks. The students will use listening, observing, and coordination skills.
- Discuss this exercise. Did the participants get nervous with the added pressure? How much did the tempo decrease?

ghoulish game (halloween)

PURPOSE:
It is difficult for any teacher to educate on some special occasions or holidays. In a perfect world, our students would be so enamored with the thought of learning about the three Bs (Bach, Beethoven, and Brahms) that they would skip the Halloween costume parade to learn more. OK … maybe that is not going to happen, but just maybe, we can sneak some learning in that day without raising suspicion.

REQUIREMENTS:
Index Cards

PREPARATION:
Mark one index card with the word, "GHOUL!"
Halloween Music (optional)
- a) "Hall of the Mountain King" (Grieg)
- b) "Toccata and Fugue in D-minor" (Bach)
- c) "Dies Irae" (from Mozart's *Requiem*)
- d) "O Fortuna" (from Orff's *Carmen Burana*)
- e) "A Night on Bald Mountain" (Mussorgsky)

DIRECTIONS:
1. Sneak the learning portion in first. Play some great "Halloween" music for your little ghosts and goblins.
2. Mark one index card with the word, "GHOUL!" The other index cards should remain blank.
3. Pass out an index card to each member of the class, making sure that the student who received the "GHOUL!" card is discreet and doesn't tell anyone else.
4. Explain that on the starting signal, students mill around the room trying to guess the existence of the GHOUL! The GHOUL will pucker and blow an air kiss of death and immediately the receiving student stages a dramatic death lasting 10 seconds.
5. Inform them the goal is to keep the identify of the GHOUL a secret so the GHOUL should try to be as secretive as possible and the victim can not indicate where the air kiss of death came from.
6. Allow students to guess who the GHOUL is, but if a guess is incorrect, they are eliminated.

VARIATION:
Students must move in the style of the music being played. Listen to the tempo and other musical elements to decide how to move around the room. This variation can be done in "ghostly pairs."

ICE TIP:
Students receive lots of candy throughout the Halloween day and night. First-year teachers, think of other ways to survive without handing out candy treats. Good luck on November 1st, the students will be on a sugar high from all the treats and tired from the late night activities. BEWARE!

thankful turkey trot

IceBreakers 2: Holiday Games – Celebrating Special Occasions

PURPOSE:
Thankful Turkey Trot is a Thanksgiving obstacle course. Students will benefit from getting to know the music room and will work on individual coordination. Great physical activity for any time of the day, especially the day before a big turkey dinner!

REQUIREMENTS:
Plenty of space
Music stands, instrument cases, chair, desks, risers and a stopwatch

PREPARATION:
Set up room before the game starts. Better yet, let students design their own obstacle course.

DIRECTIONS:
1. Allow two teams to compete concurrently.
2. Explain that this is an old-fashioned obstacle course with a turkey theme! Both teams' students must get through the obstacle course. The team with the best time wins.
3. Warn them if an item is touched or moved, the student is disqualified.
4. Track the teams' times.
5. Play music with a theme of thankfulness and encourage the students to move in the same style and the correct tempo.
6. When finished with the Turkey Trot, take a minute and reflect on Thanksgiving blessings. Students can voice the thankful thoughts or write them down for reflection.
7. Allow several minutes at the end of the icebreaker for room cleanup.

VARIATIONS:
- Be creative in the obstacle course setup, but always consider safety first. Students could crawl under chairs, step over chairs, circle a music stand three times, hop over an instrument case, walk backwards down the risers, or spin around in the teacher's chair (OK, maybe not, but you get the point). Have fun.
- This is a great game to play outside as well. Before going outside, check the terrain.

ICE TIP:
This activity builds coordination, physical endurance, flexibility (if you can't go under, you may have to go around or over the risers), and adds some healthy competition in the classroom. Students who struggle with some aspects in your class may do well with the **Turkey Trot** game. Students will become increasingly more aware of their surroundings and that is always a good thing.

TO A SPECIAL MUSIC TEACHER –
My thankful thoughts for all you do throughout the entire calendar year. You contribute to our world with your gifts of patience, knowledge, and understanding. You seek the inner light in each of your students, and they are blessed. You foster the development of each one's unique talents, understanding that intelligence cannot always be measured by ways of man. You teach one day at a time, knowing that students have good days and bad, and with this act of love, you contribute to their spiritual growth. You make a difference in so many! For your contribution to our world, thank you.
-Marci Struzinski, author

PURPOSE:

A white elephant gift exchange is a simple and inexpensive approach allowing students to bring items from their homes or share a gift from the heart. Students can bring a small bite-size candy bar, write poems, create a coupon book for a friend (I'll carry your books, a "get out of trouble with me" card, I'll clean out your spit valves, or I'll trade my lunch one day). Students must listen, or they will not be able to complete the game.

REQUIREMENTS:

Space to form one or two circles
CD player or iPod
Any music that talks about giving (My personal favorite is Sandi Patty's song "The Gift Goes On.")

PREPARATION:

Send home a note for parents explaining the white elephant gift exchange. Designate a specific day.

DIRECTIONS:

1. If bringing white elephant gifts from home, ask students to form a circle of ladies and a circle of young men.
2. Each student holds a wrapped inexpensive or silly gift. Inform them to include a brief message and a note card on the inside of the wrapped gift.
3. For our purposes, ask students to listen for two key words, "present" and "gift" in the Sandi Patty song "The Gift Goes On".
4. Each time the word "present" is sung, the gift is passed to the left. Each time the word "gift" is sung, the gift is passed to the right.
5. When the music ends, the gift in your arms is yours to open.

VARIATIONS FOR OTHER DECEMBER HOLIDAYS:

- **Celebrating Hanukkah** "Hanukkah Song" Pass the gift or a candle when a predetermined word is mentioned.
- **Celebrating Kwanzaa** Kwanzaa song and use each of the seven principles to pass a gift.
- **Other Celebrations** Use musical and holiday variations as needed.

ICE TIPS:

- White elephant gift ideas: costume jewelry, old CDs, toys, plants, hair accessories, magazines, old music books, guitar picks, books, stuffed animals, etc.
- For teacher's eyes only: In the song, "The Gift Goes On," the word "present" is mentioned three times and the word "gift" is mentioned 32 times.

holiday parade

IceBreakers 2: Holiday Games – Celebrating Special Occasions

PURPOSE:
This is a great opportunity to let students be as creative as possible with newspaper, duct tape, and other ordinary everyday items. Students work together as a team to create a costume for the assigned holiday,

REQUIREMENTS:
Old newspapers
Duct tape
Ribbon, bows, feathers, streamers, toilet paper, balloons (optional)

PREPARATION:
Prepare a list of months and/or holidays:
- January – New Year's Day, Martin Luther King, Jr. Celebration
- February – Valentine's Day, President's Day, Groundhog's Day
- March – St. Patrick's, Spring
- April – Easter, April Fools' Day, Earth Day, Administrative Assistant's Day
- May – Memorial Day, Mother's Day
- June – Father's Day, Flag Day
- July – Independence Day
- August – End of Summer, County Fairs, Birthdays
- September – Labor Day, Grandparents' Day
- October – Halloween
- November – Thanksgiving, Veteran's Day
- December – Kwanzaa, Christmas, Hanukkah, New Year's Eve

DIRECTIONS:
1. Assign each small group a month or an actual holiday.
2. Determine an allotted amount of time to collectively design a costume that represents the assigned holiday or the month.
3. Choose theme music to go with the costume and the holiday (i.e. New Year's Eve would be "Auld Lang Syne," Halloween's theme song could be "Monster Mash," and Labor Day could be celebrated with the song, "Workin' for a Livin").
4. Let students parade around the school to showcase the costumes.

VARIATIONS:
- **Calendar Club** Take pictures and make a calendar. This could be a great fundraiser for the music department.
- **Faculty Photos** Find a faculty and administrator volunteer to get "wrapped up" in the project. Let them know it is for a good cause. Make sure they approve any photos released to the public.

ICE TIP:
How do we celebrate the most important days of the year? Most people celebrate with music and food. After the costume parade, enjoy themed or holiday treats.

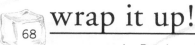 # wrap it up!

68

PURPOSE:
This is a great holiday party icebreaker or to celebrate the "birthday of the month." The challenge of this game is to get students to communicate and work as couples. If they work together, mission accomplished!

REQUIREMENTS:
One small box for each couple, filled with little goodies
Wrapping paper
Tape
Gift card
Ribbon

PREPARATION:
Place supplies (wrapping paper, small box, tape, gift card, and one ribbon) at each station. Use space on desks, floor space, or desk space for the activity. Each couple needs enough room to move around and not be frustrated by space issues.

DIRECTIONS:
1. Pair classmates who could benefit from working with one another.
2. Tell students to report to one of the stations that has supplies.
3. On the cue, "Wrap it up," students place right hands behind their backs and try to work together to gift wrap the package. Communication is the key to this icebreaker.
4. The final step is for the pair to tie a ribbon around the box (with their right one behind their back).
5. The couple who finishes wrapping the gift and writing a note on the gift card first, wins the gift wrap race.
6. When the gifts are wrapped, two couples team together to exchange gifts (each couple's station had a sticky note with the name of two other students on the note. This is the couple they will make the gift card for and wrap the package.
7. Students can choose to take the presents to a homeless shelter to share with less fortunate children. This will be a lasting gift for everyone.

VARIATION:
To add another element to the game, blindfold one of the wrappers. This will truly be a challenge!

ICE TIP:
This activity is great to use for a holiday class party. It is fun to do with all ages; even faculty members at an in-service would enjoy this team-building activity.

50 suggested song and dance titles for "move it out"

IceBreakers 2: 64 MORE Games and Fun Activities

- Thriller (Michael Jackson's famous "thriller-walk" with monster hands)
- Y-M-C-A! (Make Y-M-C-A alphabet letters with arms overhead)
- Chicken Dance (four beaks w/fingers, four elbow flaps, wiggle bottom, and four claps)
- Head, Shoulders, Knees and Toes (Reach for body parts, starting with the head)
- We Represent the Lollipop Guild (from "The Wizard of Oz"- On knees kicking sharply)
- Stop! In the Name of Love (Supremes – R palm shoots out and then draw a heart with index fingers)
- We Will, We Will Rock You (stomp, stomp, clap, and continue)
- Macarena (wrap waist, unwrap hands to hips, wrap shoulders, arms out, circle overhead)
- Do the Twist! (Chubby Checker – twist hips up and down)
- Soldja Boy (Superman, and bent wrist flick)
- Cupid Shuffle (Cupid – To the right, to the right, to the left, to the left, now kick, now walk)
- Austin Powers Theme (two fingers over eyes moving right, switch to left hand – '60s style)
- Hand Jive (from "Grease" – slap thighs twice, two claps, two switching hands, two pounding fists and thumbs)
- Greased Lightnin' (from "Grease" – fan R index finger L to R, reach up and out)
- The Hokey Pokey (put your right hand in, put your right hand out, right hand in and shake it all about)
- The Star-Spangled Banner (hand over heart, stand tall, chin lifted as if looking at the American flag)
- Do the Hustle! (Bus stop/hustle routine from '70s)
- Do the Locomotion (Make train move by circling arms)
- Baby, it's Cold Outside (Hug self and shiver like it is cold outside)
- Patty cake, patty cake, baker's man. Bake me a cake as fast as you can. (Clap hands, nursery rhyme style)
- The Wheels on the Bus Go Round and Round (Nursery rhyme - roll fists)
- Cotton-Eyed Joe (Country line dance - two kicks and polka back and repeat)
- One Singular Sensation, Every Little Move She Makes (Hold "top hat" & do Chorus Line kicks)
- Plop, Plop, Fizz, Fizz, Oh What a Relief It Is (Alka-Seltzer®, look miserable and hold tummy)
- Electric Slide (Step together, step touch, roll arms & throw down, back up)

50 suggested song and dance titles for "move it out"

- Rock-a-bye Baby in the Tree Top (Rock arms as if putting baby to sleep)
- Addams Family (na na na na, cross arms over chest, and two snaps)
- Amen... (Prayer hands)
- I'm Singin' in the Rain! (Gene Kelly – hold umbrella and splash pretend rain w/feet)
- Let's Go Fly a Kite (Mary Poppins – hold on to kite string and look up)
- Night Fever - Ah, ah, ah, ah, Stayin' Alive! Stayin' Alive! (Disco points a la Travolta)
- Jaws ("Jaws" theme – scary, make shark jaws with elbows)
- Lone Ranger (swing cowboy hat – Hi Ho, Silver!)
- Rollin' Down the River (Tina Turner-style shake hair and bend over, jogging feet)
- Can Can (Offenbach – link up and can can kicks)
- Vogue (Madonna – frame face several times and different ways with L fingers)
- Shout, a Little Bit Softer Now (Blue's Brothers – reach arms up and then get small)
- Skater's Waltz (Pretend to be skating with a partner – slowly on the ice, muff on hands)
- Aaay! (The Fonz's greeting from the "Happy Days" TV show – thumbs up)
- At the Copa, Copacabana (Barry Manilow – roll hands and then flip to Latin snap)
- Here I Come to Save the Day (Mighty Mouse cartoon character - hands on hips, chest up)
- M-i-c-k-e-y M-o-u-s-e (Disney® – make mouse ears)
- Wipe Out! (ride a surfboard and pretend to balance and then wipe-out by falling on floor)
- If You're Happy and You Know It Clap Your Hands (make a smiley face and two claps)
- Bye, bye, bye (*NSync – puppet routine, use right fingers and pinch them together three)
- Charleston (Touch right foot front, step, touch left foot back and step)
- Itsy Bitsy Spider (Index finger to thumb and alternate to simulate crawling)
- Mr. Roboto (Robot moves that are very tight and jerky)
- Shake Your Groove Thing (Shake hips back and forth)
- Mexican Hat Dance (Pretend to throw a hat on the ground and rapidly circle the hat by stomping feet and clapping hands)

"Dance as if no one were watching. Sing as if no one were listening.
And live every day as if it were your last."
~Anonymous (based on words by Souza)

notes

IceBreakers 2: 64 MORE Games and Fun Activities

Valerie Lippoldt Mack, lead instructor of music at Butler Community College in El Dorado, Kansas, received a Bachelor of Arts from Bethany College, a Bachelor of Music Education and Masters of Music Education from Wichita State University. Valerie has gained experience and recognition as a music educator and professional choreographer throughout the United States. Her choreography has been featured at Carnegie Hall, Disney World, national ACDA conventions and MENC workshops. A noted clinician, adjudicator, and director, she has presented and adjudicated more than 500 workshops and festivals. She and her husband Tom, direct the annual Butler Showchoir Showcase each summer in El Dorado, Kansas.

At Butler Community College, Valerie directs the 100-voice Butler Concert Choir, the Butler Headliners Showchoir, the Smorgaschords Barbershop Quartet, and teaches tap dance and private voice. The barbershop quartet continuously places at the International Collegiate Barbershop Competition. Valerie was honored as the Butler Master Teacher, has delivered commencement addresses, and is in demand as a motivational speaker.

In her spare time, Valerie teaches at the Kansas Dance Academy, directs the Risen Savior Lutheran Church Choir, is a talent coach for the Miss America program, and is involved with family activities. Valerie and Tom reside in Wichita, Kansas with their two children, Stevie and Zane.

Olympic Games for the Music Classroom (MO751) This collection of musical games with an Olympic theme was created by Valerie Lippoldt Mack and Todd Schreiber. At the sound of the starting pistol, the competition begins with rhythm-reading, note values, rest values, note names, movement and listening games, as well as physical games that will bring out the best in your music athletes!

Icebreakers: 60 Fun Activities to Build a Better Choir (MO750) includes favorite team-building activities and fun games to teach life lessons of respect, tolerance and patience, as well as encourage students to be positive, focus-minded musicians.

Shawnee Press

EXCLUSIVELY DISTRIBUTED BY HAL LEONARD CORPORATION

www.shawneepress.com